Hospice Tails

The Animal Companions Who Journey With Hospice Patients and Their Families

Hospice Tails

The Animal Companions Who Journey
With Hospice Patients and Their Families

Debra Stang

Table of Contents

Table of Contents

Foreword

I stopped my car about five blocks away from the address listed on my official-looking agency folder and nervously ran my hands up and down my legs, leaving sweat stains on my new silk pants. That ought to make a great impression on my first client. I battled the urge to run home and change clothes, or maybe just run home and hide under the covers until the school of social work dropped me from its roster.

I was in the first week of my MSW program and on my way to meet my first-ever client. All social work students had to do internships, or practicums. My practicum placement was at a mental health center, and my job was getting out in the community to do case management with personality-disordered clients, the clients no one else wanted to work with.

It didn't help that the more experienced case managers referred to the other student who had been assigned to the agency and I as "fresh meat."

Well, being late wasn't going to get me off to a good start. I forced myself to put the car into drive and found the address more quickly than I had hoped. The house was covered with peeling white siding, and a metal fence surrounded the front yard. I put my hand on the fence and was greeted with a tremendous *WHOOF* as a Great Dane came charging around the side of the house.

I backed away, hoping that if I maintained the fiction that he couldn't jump that gate with one leg tied behind his back, he would, too. Why, oh why, had I ever thought I wanted to be a social worker? I'd been a data entry clerk before. It really wasn't such a bad job.

The Great Dane glared at me and barked some more. I was about two seconds from getting back in my car—fresh meat was one thing, but dog food was something else entirely—when a tired-looking woman opened the front door to the house and roared, "Baby, hush!" She turned unfriendly eyes on me. "Whadda you want? I already told you I sent my son to school today. If he didn't get there, that's not my problem."

"No, no," I called over the fence. "I'm not from your son's school. I'm your case manager. From the mental health center."

The woman stared at me with bloodshot eyes. She was wearing a pink robe that came down to mid-thigh, and, as far as I could tell, nothing else. "They said I had to let you in if I wanted to get my medicine," she said, opening the door a little bit.

Nice. I mentally cursed the unknown psychiatrist who had used me as a bargaining chip. How was I supposed to build a relationship with a client who was only tolerating me so she could get her prescriptions filled?

"I said come in," she told me, a little louder.

I looked at the dog.

"Don't worry about him. He won't touch you…unless I tell him to." She grinned at me with coffee-stained teeth.

I tried to smile back and walked through the gate. Baby grumbled low in his throat but stayed flat on the ground. I walked up to the porch and held my hand out to the woman. "Hi, I'm Debra."

"Leigh," she said, taking my hand without much enthusiasm. "How old are you?"

She caught me off guard. "Twenty-six."

Leigh groaned and slapped a hand to her forehead. "I fucking need real help, and they give me a kid to babysit."

According to her chart, which I had practically memorized, she was only 29, herself. I followed her into the house and sat carefully on the rickety chair she pointed at. She went to the kitchen to get herself a cup of coffee. She didn't offer to get me one.

My voice a little squeaky with nerves, I started telling her the ways I could help her navigate community resources and problem-solve any issues that were troubling her.

She came back into the living room, sat down on the couch, and fixed me with a flat, unfriendly look.

Just then, a hamster darted out from under the couch, ran across the living room floor, and scrambled under the closet door.

It happened so quickly, I wasn't positive I'd seen it. I gulped and kept talking about the case management program.

Leigh yawned loudly.

Three minutes later, the hamster made another appearance, this time scampering out of the closet into a hole in one of the cabinets. A few minutes later, cheeks bulging with purloined food, he made for the closet again.

"Why is there a hamster running around the house?" I couldn't help asking.

"He's a fucking guard dog, what do you think?"

I didn't say anything. I couldn't think of anything to say. I just hoped I didn't cry.

Leigh sighed. "Actually, he belongs to my kid. He got out of his cage, and I can't catch him, and I'm afraid one of the cats is going to eat him, and then my kid will hate me even worse than he does already. Happy?"

"I can help you catch your hamster," I said.

She smirked at me.

"No, seriously, I used to have hamsters for pets. They were always getting out of their cages."

For the first time, something that wasn't contempt glimmered in her eyes. "I don't have money…"

"All you need is a trash can with smooth sides, a pile of books or magazines, and some sunflower seeds."

"That I've got."

I showed Leigh how to set a simple trap for the runaway hamster by putting sunflower seeds at the bottom of a shallow wastebasket and building a makeshift ladder of books to the top. When the hamster slid down to get the sunflower seeds, he wouldn't be able to climb back up the smooth sides of the basket, and he'd be stuck there.

I also looked over the hamster's cage and showed Leigh how to reinforce the most likely escape points.

By then, our time was up, so I left.

I didn't expect much when I called her the next morning, but she was delighted. "That trash can thingy you showed me yesterday worked! When Darrin and I woke up this morning, the hamster was running around the bottom of the can, and his cheeks were stuffed with sunflower seeds. We put Mr. Smarty right back into his cage, and that's where he'll stay."

Her voice got softer. "When we found him this morning, Darrin hugged me. He ain't hugged me in almost a year."

"That's great," I said.

She was quiet for a moment. "Look, I know I was pretty mean to you yesterday, but I've got this paperwork from the court to fill out. Darrin's father's a mean bastard, and if I get the paperwork done, the lady at the court told me I could get an order of protection. But I don't read so good…"

I went over and helped her get the protective order. We got along great for the rest of the year.

I've loved animals all my life, so it's hardly surprising that a hamster figured into my first successful clinical experience.

Throughout my career, I've worked with clients who didn't care if they had food in their own refrigerators but who would rob a bank to make sure their dog or their cat ate properly.

A homeless man I worked with for two years tore at my heart by carrying his pet lizard around on his shoulder wherever he went. When he asked for money, he never asked for himself. "I can eat out of the trash," he said. "You wouldn't believe the good stuff restaurants throw away. But Ichabod here needs a special diet from the vet, or he'll die. I don't suppose you could…?"

I always did.

When I started working at a hospice with patients who were facing death and with their loved ones, I discovered that the animals in their lives assumed roles of mammoth proportions. Animals were the calmers, the comforters, the counselors, the best friends, the extra dose of pain medicine when it was most needed, and sometimes, the comic relief.

In my time as a hospice social worker, I've met dogs, cats, hamsters, mice, guinea pigs, horses, fish, and even the odd snake. Each one of these special animals was deeply attached to a very special human.

I write this book to honor the stories and the journeys of all my clients, both of the two-legged and the four-legged variety.

Because strict health privacy laws ensure that information passed between a client and social worker is privileged, I've taken some liberties with the facts. I've changed names, details, and species to protect the privacy of my clients. But I haven't changed the underlying truths. Each bond I've described between human and animal actually existed.

Undoubtedly, some people will see this as a sad book because it deals with the reality of lives that are ending. I, however, see it as a joyous celebration of the best humankind—and animal kind—has to offer. And if *Hospice Tails* brings a tear to your eye, I hope it also brings a smile to your lips.

The first of the hospice pets you're going to meet is King and the tough-as-nails human who rescued him from a life of abuse.

Chapter One
The World's Biggest Lap Dog

The information on the referral form from the home health agency was brief and bleak. I had been a hospice social worker long enough to interpret the hopelessness and frustration behind it. "Sixty-eight year old female. Pancreatic cancer with metastases to bone and liver. Poor pain control. Supportive family. Beware of dog."

I blinked and re-read that last sentence. *Beware of dog?* That was a new one.

Later that day, when I called the patient's daughter, Nancy, to set up an initial visit, I asked her about the allegedly dangerous dog. She burst into tears. "Please don't make Mama get rid of King. It would kill her. It would kill all of us. He's part of the family."

"Of course I won't make you get rid of your dog," I said. "I just have to make sure our staff is safe when we come to the home to make visits. What kind of dog is it?"

"A pit bull."

Great. "About how big would you say?"

"Oh, King's a big boy. Probably close to a hundred pounds."

Double great. Why couldn't they have had a nasty tempered Shih Tzu? "Isn't that pretty big for a pit bull?" I said, hoping she was exaggerating.

A long pause greeted my optimistic question. "Well, um...the vet thinks King might be part Rottweiler, too. We're not sure."

"Listen," I said to the daughter, "maybe you should just put King in another room while we visit."

"It wouldn't work," she said. "He hates being separated from Mama. He'll bark and howl and jump at the door until we let him out. I think he could *break* that door."

This was just getting better and better.

"Well, how about putting him on a leash?" I said. "Just at first, until he gets to know us." *And gets it through his thick head that nurse, hospice aide, social worker, and chaplain are not food groups.*

"Until he gets to know you!" the daughter said. "That's exactly the problem."

"I beg your pardon?"

"That home health agency, the one that told us to call you...they sent a physical therapist over to try to help Mama get stronger. He was so rude he didn't even introduce himself, didn't even look at me or my brothers. He just walked over to the couch and started moving Mama's arms and legs. That cancer is in her bones now, and it hurt so bad she couldn't help screaming, and King, he was just trying to protect her..." her voice trailed off.

I winced in sympathy, and not for the physical therapist. For the first time I dared to hope that King and I might get along after all. "I'm so sorry that happened to your mother," I said. "We'll do things very differently, I promise."

A few hours later, I got to meet King in person when the nurse and I went to the patient's home to admit her to hospice services.

The patient's name was Lisa. She lived in a small, clean house with her daughter Nancy, a jittery woman in her forties, who bounced from one foot to the other while she shook hands with me and the nurse. I could easily imagine her channeling all that excess energy into cleaning frenzies. No wonder the place was immaculate.

Lisa's three other adult children, all boys, hovered around the periphery, wanting to help but not sure exactly how to go about it. One of them wiped silent tears from his cheeks every few seconds. Another held King on a thick leash.

And then there was King himself, who greeted us with thunderous barking and growling that made conversation with the patient and the family nearly impossible. King was every bit as big as Nancy had said. He was a uniform tan color with the squat, powerful build typical of the breed and ice-water eyes that never wavered from me and the nurse. I could all but hear him calculating exactly how many bites it would take to finish each of us off, and how deep a hole he would have to dig to hide the bodies.

But all those thoughts flew from my mind the moment I saw Lisa. She was in torment. She had curled herself into a small ball of misery on the couch, and was rocking back and forth with her hands pressed against her abdomen. "It just hurts so much," was all she could say when I leaned down to talk to her.

While I went over hospice with the family, shouting to make myself heard over King's barking, and got some legal paperwork signed, the nurse immediately got on the phone with Lisa's doctor to get some stronger pain medication ordered. At first the doctor was hesitant. "I've never prescribed narcotics at that dosage," he said. "Is it even legal?"

The nurse explained that the dosage she was requesting was perfectly legal and that hospice would be visiting Lisa regularly to make sure she didn't have any ill effects from the medication. Skeptical, but willing to do whatever he could to help his patient, Lisa's doctor approved the medication.

Now all we could do was wait for the pharmacy to deliver it.

The nurse, who had grown up around pit bulls, stretched out her hand to within a few feet of King's nose so he could catch her scent. He attempted to lunge at her, but Lisa's son held the leash tight.

The nurse ignored King and went to Lisa. "I need to check some vital signs," she said softly. "I'll do my best not to hurt you. Is that okay?"

Lisa nodded wearily.

The nurse was as gentle as possible, but Lisa whimpered a little when the blood pressure cuff tightened around her arm. King's ears went up, and his barking took on a whole new intensity.

The family and I spoke soothing words, and the youngest son slipped him a treat. He continued to give the nurse the evil eye.

"Poor King," I said. "This must be so hard for you. So hard for all of you."

The wait for the medication to arrive seemed interminable, but in fact it was only about forty-five minutes. The nurse gave Lisa her first dose of Roxanol, a type of liquid morphine that goes under the tongue or in the pocket of the cheek and is directly absorbed into the membranes of the mouth. It worked quickly, and Lisa's moaning soon ceased.

King, finally, was quiet as well.

A few minutes later, Lisa stopped hugging her abdomen.

"Oh thank God, thank God," Nancy whispered. "It's working."

A half hour passed and the nurse gave Lisa another dose of Roxanol as well as a dose of long-acting pain medication. Lisa was relaxed and sleepy now. I went to the couch and sat down cross-legged on the floor "Oh, Lisa," I said, "I'm so glad your pain is better."

She smiled, nodded, and squeezed my hand.

About that time, I caught movement out of the corner of my eye. King was rushing towards me. The son who had been holding the leash had been so caught up in watching his mother that he had let the leash slip through his fingers. There was no time to get out of King's way, so I just sat there and wondered through the icy panic fogging my brain what it would feel like to be eaten by a pit bull.

King reached me in two leaps, charged between me and Lisa, turned his broad back to me…and then plopped his butt squarely down on my lap.

The room exploded in laughter. "Oh, King, don't be so silly," giggled Lisa. "You're the world's biggest lap dog." I scratched King behind his ears and breathed a sigh of relief. Life was going to be much easier in this household with King as an ally rather than an enemy.

The nurse and I stayed for another half hour to make sure that Lisa's pain really was controlled and that the family understood how to give her the medicine. They did, and assured us that they would use the medication regularly so Lisa would never have to be in so much pain again.

While Lisa was on service with hospice, I visited her about twice a month to provide emotional support to her and her family. As I sat on the floor by Lisa's couch—she had refused to allow us to get her a hospital bed—King always perched firmly on my lap, just keeping an eye on things.

Lisa had not had an easy life. Her husband had abandoned her with four small children, and she had had to work two and sometimes three jobs at a time to raise them, but she was proud of her hard work and of how richly it had paid off. She and Nancy loved sharing stories about the things they had done as a family.

King had come along three years ago. Lisa was leaving the diner where she worked as a waitress when she saw a young man with dreadlocks and a leather jacket kicking a cringing puppy. It never occurred to Lisa to be afraid. Her years as a single mother had taught her to protect those weaker than herself.

She darted between the young man and the puppy, using every ounce of her 100-pound, 5'1" body to push King's tormentor away from his victim. "You bully! You monster! You…" She called the young man a few more names that he probably hadn't expected to come out of the mouth of a 65-year old woman. Then she scooped the trembling puppy into her arms and stalked away.

"Hey, bitch!" the man called after her. "That dog cost me a hundred bucks."

"You should have thought of that before you beat him," Lisa said. "He's mine, now. Or we can always call the police and let them decide."

Lisa always chuckled at this point in the story. "I guess that fellow remembered somewhere else he needed to be, because as soon as I said the word police, all that was left of him was his ugly backside running in the opposite direction."

"Mama, you could have been hurt," Nancy reproved her, but with a smile.

King got up and licked Lisa's face. She pretended to push him away. "King, you have doggy breath." Then she relented and gave him a tight hug.

Unfortunately, Lisa's cancer was very aggressive. She had only been on service with hospice for three months before she entered what we refer to as the active dying process. This means that the body has started the process of shutting itself down, and that death is only a few days or hours away.

I increased my visits to support Lisa's grieving family. That family, of course, included King. As soon as I came through the door, he nudged me gently but firmly onto the floor beside Lisa's couch. Then he sat on my lap. I had to coax, beg, bribe, and finally physically push him off of me when it was time for me to end my visits.

Even at her weakest, Lisa still found the energy to give King a pat on the head when he anxiously pawed at her arm.

The night before Lisa died, she lapsed into a brief coma and stopped responding to everything around her, even King.

By that morning, when I got to the house, her breathing had started to change, speeding up and then slowing down. Soon there were long pauses in between each breath. About an hour later, she took a last deep gasp and her chest stopped moving.

We waited in silence for several moments. Then the hospice nurse said softly, "I'm so sorry. She's gone."

Nancy cried out and fell to her knees. One of her brothers bent down to comfort her. Another slammed his fist into the wall. The third just stood there with tears running down his face. King threw his head back and let loose a howl of sheer anguish and desolation.

The nurse and I both said and did whatever we could to ease the pain in the room, but some hurt runs far too deep for words to touch. Nancy and I sat together on the floor beside Lisa's couch until the funeral home arrived to remove Lisa's body. King sat on my lap and whimpered uncertainly while I held him and rocked him like the abused puppy he had once been.

We buried Lisa on one of those rare, spring-like days that sometimes pop up out of nowhere in the middle of winter. King attended the graveside service. As soon as he saw me, he let out one of his overpowering barks, charged over to me, and butted his head against my legs until I sat down hard in the wet grass. Then he climbed on my lap. "The world's biggest lap dog," I whispered in his ear.

I've never much believed in life after death, but I knew that Lisa and her family did. And I also knew that if Lisa was watching us from somewhere far away, she was laughing.

Chapter Two
Sometimes They Stop Purring

The first sound I heard when I entered the home to meet my new client was the sound of a contented cat. Loud purring and an occasional, "Mrrroooow," filled the entry way as I shook hands with the patient's husband, Bill.

"Come meet my wife," he said, leading me down a few steps into a sunken living room. Large windows on all sides let the warm spring sunshine flow into the room. Bill's wife, my patient, was seated comfortably in a recliner in the corner. A soft blue blanket covered her knees. The cat that was making all the happy noises was curled into a ball on her lap.

The woman smiled up at me near-sightedly. "Well, hello. Where have you been? I've missed you."

"This is Mary," Bill said quietly. "She's had Alzheimer's for about five years now."

The cat continued to purr madly, showing no signs of fear at my approach. I crouched down by the woman's chair and offered her my hand. "Hi, Mary, I'm Debra. I'm going to be coming to visit you. Is that okay?"

As the woman took my hand with cold fingers, I noticed something odd about the cat—it wasn't real. It was made of plastic covered with soft, synthetic fur, and the purring and meowing were controlled by batteries.

I glanced up at Bill. He smiled sheepishly. "She's always loved cats," he said, "but we could never have one because I'm so allergic." For a moment, tears shimmered in his warm brown eyes, but he blinked them away and continued steadily, "She doesn't know the difference, now."

I looked back at Mary. She hummed under her breath as she rhythmically stroked the cat's back. "You love your kitty, don't you?" I asked her.

She nodded proudly. "Kitty."

"I think she's just beautiful," I said. "I've always loved cats, too."

Mary and Bill both beamed at me.

Although Mary suffered from Alzheimer's, her hospice diagnosis was "adult failure to thrive." This occurs when a patient with several medical conditions starts losing weight and declining in other ways, not due to any one condition, but to a deadly combination of all of them. In addition to her Alzheimer's, Mary also carried the diagnoses of heart disease, diabetes, and the early stages of renal failure.

But her most significant problem, at least as far as Bill was concerned, was her devastating cognitive decline. About a year earlier, she had started losing track of where she was. She begged Bill to take her home. When he wouldn't—couldn't—because they were already at home, she screamed, sobbed, and called him names. "Language I didn't even think she knew," Bill told me grimly.

He had tried everything the doctor suggested to bring Mary's erratic behavior under control, but sedatives only made her more agitated, and even strong anti-psychotic medications didn't calm her. Then one day, while waiting in line at the pharmacy, he saw the toy cat and picked it up on a whim.

"I never thought she'd think it was real," Bill said, "But she took it right into her lap and started petting it, and it started purring and meowing like it does and…well, she's been a lot calmer ever since."

As the summer passed, Mary continued to decline slowly. She grew too weak to use her walker and started to get around in a wheelchair. And wherever she went, Kitty purred and meowed on her lap.

Mary was perfectly content, but the strain was beginning to tell on Bill. His face took on a gray, haunted look, and he, too, began to lose an alarming amount of weight.

I offered to set up a meeting with our volunteer coordinator to arrange for a volunteer to sit with Mary while Bill took some time for himself, but he brushed that suggestion aside. He also refused when I offered to place Mary in a nursing home for a few days while he rested and perhaps even went out of town to visit some of his children from his first marriage.

"In sickness and in health," he told me. "Isn't that what I promised?"

"But you're making your*self* sick, and there's no reason for it, not when so many resources are available…"

He patted my hand and shook his head. "I'll manage."

Two weeks later, he met me at the door when I stopped by to make my regular visit. His hands were trembling and tears stood in his eyes. I heard no sound from Mary's corner chair. "Oh, Debra, I've done something terrible," he whispered.

Every horror story I'd ever heard about caregivers who snapped and hurt or even killed their loved ones raced through my mind. Bill was one of the gentlest men I'd ever met. But still…

"What's happened?" I asked, forcing myself to speak calmly.

He unclenched a trembling hand and showed me four AA batteries. "I killed Kitty," he said. "It was driving me insane. Purring and meowing all day and all night. *Every* day and *every* night." He rubbed the bridge of his nose with his free hand.

I wanted to laugh from sheer relief, but poor Bill looked so wretched that I didn't dare. "That isn't anything so terrible, Bill," I said instead. "You didn't hurt yourself. You didn't hurt Mary. Those would have been terrible things. Taking the batteries out of a toy cat is not the end of the world. Does Mary notice the difference?"

Bill swallowed hard. "She…she said Kitty seemed awfully quiet today."

"Did it bother her?"

He shook his head. "No. I didn't know what to say, so I just told her cats stop purring so much when they got older. She seemed to accept that."

When I approached Mary, she looked no different than she had on every other occasion when I'd visited her. She greeted me with a cheerful smile and offered me her right hand while she continued to pet the now-silent Kitty with her left.

I tried to chat with her, but she could only say a word or two at a time that made sense before she started stringing random words together in a speech pattern known as "word salad." She continued to smile, though, and showed no signs of distress. I patted her hand and stood up to leave.

"Kitty's quiet today," she said out of nowhere, the first coherent sentence I'd heard her speak in over a month.

I crouched back down beside her. "Yes. I noticed that, too."

"Sometimes when they get older they stop purring," she said. "That—he—that man—he told me that."

"He's right," I said.

She nodded, closed her eyes, and continued to stroke the soft white fur.

Mary turned out to be one of our "hospice saves." About a month after Kitty stopped purring, Mary's appetite improved, and she soon regained all the weight she'd lost and then some. She even started using her walker again. Her memory, unfortunately, did not get better, but it looked like she could live in her present state for many more years.

Tears mingled with laughter the day we had to discharge Mary from hospice care.

"We're always here if she gets worse again and you need us," I told Bill, "and I'll stay in touch just to make sure things are going okay."

I have stayed in touch. I call Bill once a month or so. He tells me Mary has become quieter and even more forgetful, but she is content to sit in her chair all day and pet Kitty. Only rarely does she speak meaningful words, but about once a week or so she announces out of nowhere, "It's the strangest thing. Sometimes they just stop purring."

Chapter Three
Cold Comfort

"I didn't even know women died from breast cancer anymore," Brandon said. His grief encased him like a block of ice. He kept his eyes averted from mine and wrapped his long arms, marked with sleeve tattoos, around his knees. "I mean they're always talking about raising funds for a cure. They've even got football players wearing *pink* for Chrissakes. Where's all that money going?"

I listened silently as he continued to express his grief and anger.

He had every reason to be sad and angry.

Six months earlier, he had been a 28-year old newlywed, freshly employed as a sous-chef at one of the nicer restaurants in the city, and he and his 26-year old wife Joanna, who worked as a server at the same restaurant, were trying to conceive their first child.

When Joanna slipped on the ice and broke her arm, neither of them thought much about it. Accidents happen, after all, and broken bones mend easily in the young. But after the doctor in the emergency department saw Joanna's x-rays, he frowned and ordered a CT scan. Then he admitted Joanna to the hospital, where she underwent another scan and several blood tests.

The evening after Joanna was admitted to the hospital, a young oncology resident stopped in to talk to her and Brandon. Joanna's arm had broken, he explained awkwardly, not because of the force of the fall, but because she had cancer in her bones. The cancer had metastasized, or spread, from a primary tumor in her breast. She was to start chemotherapy immediately.

When the resident left the room, he assumed that Joanna and Brandon understood that Joanna's prognosis was extremely poor. In truth, they understood no such thing. Neither of them had a medical background, and as far as they were concerned, breast cancer was curable.

The next five months brought one futile treatment after another. Joanna's cancer continued to spread throughout her gaunt body, and she seemed to grow weaker and more tired by the day. Brandon and Joanna tried to keep each other's spirits up by telling each other that chemotherapy makes everyone tired and sick, but even they were starting to suspect Joanna was fighting a battle she couldn't win.

Their worst fears were confirmed when, after a stay in the hospital, a doctor asked them bluntly where Joanna wanted to die.

"I--At home, I guess," Brandon stammered, unable to believe the choice that had been dropped into their laps so abruptly.

The hospital arranged for hospice care, and Joanna went home the following day. The hospice nurse and I met with her and Brandon, got legal paperwork signed, and completed a quick initial assessment. Joanna died that night, while a disbelieving Brandon clasped her hand and begged her to stay just a little longer.

Since my involvement with them had been so brief, I was surprised when Brandon accepted my offer of bereavement support, but he had a lot that he needed to get off his chest. I had been at the house he and Joanna had once shared for over an hour, and he had been talking non-stop the entire time.

When the words finally ran out, he and I sat quietly together, contemplating the tragic loss of such a young woman.

"I'm empty," he said softly. "Food tastes like cardboard. I don't want to get up in the mornings. I feel like I've forgotten how to laugh. A guy at work asked me if I was going to start dating again, and I almost punched him. What's wrong with me?"

"You're grieving," I said simply. "And it hurts like hell. But everything that you're feeling is perfectly normal."

More silence as Brandon absorbed this. I gave him a few minutes and then asked gently, "Are there any times when you feel less sad than others? Is there anything that eases the pain a little?"

His eyes brightened the tiniest bit. "Yeah," he said, "Demeter."

"Demeter?"

"Joanna and I had a lot of pets, but she was always my favorite. Joanna's, too. Wait a minute. I'll show you." He jumped up and ran into a back room.

Normally, one of the first things I assess is whether the patient and his or her family have any pets, but Joanna had been on service such a short time, I hadn't had a chance to ask that question. I was glad

Brandon had an animal companion, though. Animals can bring so much comfort during the grieving process.

I had recently spoken on the phone with a woman whose mother had been practically catatonic after her husband died. She remained profoundly depressed until a stray cat found its way to her door. She let it in, nursed it back to health, spoiled it rotten, and her depression resolved practically overnight. The daughter was amazed. "Here I was dragging her to all these therapy appointments, when all she really needed was a pet," the daughter had told me.

I was still smiling as I remembered that story when Brandon came out of the back room.

When I saw what he had with him, though, my stomach felt as if the ground had fallen out from underneath me. Wrapped around Brandon's arm was a three-foot long red and orange snake with bright red eyes. I've never been fond of reptiles, snakes least of all. Every instinct in my body urged me to jump to my feet and back away.

But I made myself sit still. Suppose, I thought, someone came into my apartment to help me? Suppose that person saw one of my beloved cats, jumped up, and screamed, *"Oh, how disgusting, get it out of here!"* Would I ever trust that person again?

Not a chance.

So I remained in the recliner and even managed to keep what I hoped was a smile on my face. "So this is Demeter," I said, hoping Brandon didn't notice how my voice creaked.

"Yeah," he said, rubbing the snake's head with his thumb. "She's an albino corn snake. I've had her about five years. She's my sweet girl. Aren't you, Demi?"

If Demeter had an answer, I didn't hear it. I did notice, though, that she seemed to raise her head against Brandon's thumb, as if she liked the sensation of being petted. *Just like my cats did when I scratched their heads.*

"Would you like to hold her?" Brandon asked.

"Uh..." I couldn't think of a polite way to say that I'd rather undergo a root canal without anesthesia. "Sure."

"Hold out your arm." He deftly unwrapped Demeter from his own arm and transferred her over to mine. My heart pounded in my chest. How the hell had this happened? How had I started out doing a routine bereavement visit and ended up holding a three-foot long albino corn snake? I tried to swallow, but couldn't get any saliva into my mouth.

Brandon was chatting the whole time, telling me about how he had been too shy to ask Joanna out until he overheard her say that she loved snakes. He invited her over to see Demeter, and then convinced her to stay and watch a movie on HBO. It was their first date.

As I listened, and as Demeter remained sedately coiled around my arm and made no move to spring at me or bite me, my panic slowly abated. I'd never held a snake before. I couldn't help noticing that she weighed more than I had expected. Her skin was cool to the touch, but not remotely slimy. In fact, it had a pleasing, dry roughness. I found myself extending a couple of fingers to stroke her head, just as Brandon had done a few minutes earlier. She responded to me the same way she had to him, pushing up against my fingers.

"Good girl," I whispered, and extended my arm slowly to give her back to Brandon.

He took her and pressed his lips briefly against the red and orange coils before settling her around his shoulders.

"I'm so glad you have her, Brandon," I said, meaning it.

He managed a small smile, his first since I'd entered the home. "Yeah, we're kind of a team. As long as I've got Demeter, I'll make it through."

Brandon did make it through. I continued to visit him for six months, until he moved out of the city. After that, he occasionally called or sent me a note to let me know how he was doing. The last I heard, he was dating again. His new girlfriend is also a chef. And she's crazy about Demeter.

Chapter Four

I Was Supposed to Go First

"Can you come over and stay with Mom this afternoon?" Jeff asked me, struggling to keep the tears from his voice.

There was no way. It was already the third week in the month, and I had clients I hadn't even seen once yet. Kim and her son Jeff lived east of the city where the traffic was always terrible.

I started to explain all this.

Jeff stopped me. "I…it's Blue. I'm going to have to have her put down."

"Oh, Jeff, not Blue! Surely there's some other way…"

"She must have had a stroke last night. This morning, she's just lying here and whimpering. Mom and I both agreed it would be best…"

"I'll be there," I said, trying to imagine Kim without Blue. I couldn't.

My first meeting with Kim, less than six months earlier, hadn't been stellar. She was in her early sixties, a registered nurse. She had served in a MASH unit in Vietnam. From there, she'd returned to Texas to step into a demanding career as a surgical nurse. Jeff was her only son, and she had never married his father. If there was any resulting scandal, it didn't faze her. Jeff grew up, got his college degree in journalism, and left home, though he stayed in touch with Kim through letters and email.

Kim continued her career as a surgical nurse, but little things were starting to bother her. She caught herself stumbling more than once. A couple of times, she even dropped surgical instruments. These incidents were embarrassing, but Kim reckoned she wasn't getting any younger. Maybe it was time for her to think about an administrative job.

In the fall of 2007, Kim's world fell apart. She was called to her supervisor's office, where the supervisor informed her that a co-worker had reported Kim for being intoxicated on the job. Luckily, the supervisor knew Kim well enough to realize that the allegation wasn't true, but he also knew something must be very wrong. He told Kim not to come back to work without a doctor's clearance.

Muttering under her breath every step of the way, Kim marched across the hospital to the office where her primary care physician practiced. He squeezed her in immediately, but within minutes, it became obvious that the doctor's routine neurological checks were not going well.

He advised Kim to take time off until she could see a neurologist. Two months later, the devastating diagnosis was confirmed. Kim had ALS, also known as Lou Gehrig's disease. ALS affects the nerve cells in the brain and spinal cord. As these cells shrivel and die, muscle function all over the body ceases. Twenty percent of people with ALS die between three and five years after diagnosis.

Kim was ready to check herself into a nursing home in Texas and wait for the inevitable, but her son wouldn't hear of it. He insisted that she come to live with him. He did his research and saw to it that she had the best doctors in the area. For the first two years, Kim seemed to hold her own, but then she had a rapid decline and it became clear that she was couldn't live much longer. Jeff contacted our hospice to care for his mother.

By the time we met Kim, she was no longer able to sign paperwork, but she had had a rubber stamp made of her signature and insisted on using that instead of having Jeff, who was her medical power of attorney, sign the hospice papers for her.

She listened with tight lips to my explanation of each form and then, carefully, set the stamp down on the area to be signed.

When we were finished, she spoke. Her voice was somewhat slurred and gravelly, but she made each word as distinct as possible. "Young lady, don't waste your time on me. I'm an atheist and have no wish to be converted to any religion. I am also not the type to weep into my tea over my misfortunes. So we will not be seeing each other again."

That was about as direct a refusal of services as I had ever heard. Still, I made one last-ditch effort. "Thank you for being honest with me. Let me tell you a little bit about myself, and then you can decide whether you want to work with me. First, I am also an atheist. Second, my job isn't to host a pity party, it's to help you find ways to do what you want for as long as you can."

She looked steadily into my eyes for several seconds. "Can you come back in a month? Perhaps we should talk some more."

A month later, I found Kim just as direct. "I'm still not sure I need your services, but you took me off guard when you said you were an atheist. I thought all you hospice people were religious."

I shrugged. "A lot of us are, but I'm not."

"What do you tell your patients who believe in God?"

"My beliefs don't come into the picture. It's their deaths, so it's their beliefs that matter. If someone wants me to sing hymns to them, I sing. If someone wants me to pray with them, I pray."

"You mean you lie," she said with the first sign of a smile I'd seen from her.

I smiled back. "I guess you could call it that. I'd rather think of it as honoring my client's journey."

"What happens when people ask you the big question, the one about life after death?"

"If they already have beliefs, I respect them. If they ask, I'm honest. I say I don't know, and I don't. I have beliefs and ideas—we all do—but that's all they are. No one has ever been back from death, true brain death, I mean, to prove or disprove anything, so we wait, and wonder."

"An atheist who likes mysteries," Kim said dryly. "Now I've seen it all. Sit down and I'll have Jeff make you a cup of tea. If you don't drink tea, you should start. It's very good for you."

I had been accepted.

It was also during this visit that I got to meet Blue. Blue was one of the funniest looking dogs I've ever had the pleasure of seeing. Her coat was such a rich black that parts of it looked blue, hence her name. Her fur was all poodle, warm and curly. But her face was smushed in like a pug's, and she had the elongated body of a miniature dachshund.

"What kind of dog is that?" I asked, trying to keep a straight face as Blue sniffed my fingers and leaned her weight against my hand so I could rub her head.

Jeff handed me my cup of tea. It tasted vile. "One of my friends breeds poodles," he explained. "About ten years ago, the latch on the purebred bitch's fence broke, and she...uh...received a gentleman caller."

"So, Blue is a mix of poodle and whatever got into the poodle's cage?"

Jeff laughed. "That's about the size of it. There were only three pups in the litter. The runt died, and my friend was going to have the other two euthanized, but I took Blue, and another guy I knew took the third one."

Blue was a friendly little dog, always eager for attention and love, and she seemed to know that Kim, for all her tough talk, needed plenty of both. She spent most of her time sitting beside Kim's electric wheelchair so Kim could reach down and pat her head. On days when Kim was so weak she couldn't even manage the wheelchair, Blue stretched out beside her in bed, pressing her body to Kim's.

Kim pretended indifference to all this, but she told me once in an unguarded moment, "I've been taking care of things all my life, and right now Blue's the only creature that has any need of me whatsoever."

"What about Jeff?"

"He doesn't need me. If anything, it's the other way around. Will you read to me some more?"

"Sure," I said, and opened the book we were reading, a novel about the third wife of Henry VIII.

Blue had always seemed like a healthy dog, and I had anticipated she would outlive Kim by many years. The phone call from Jeff was shattering. My heart ached as I made the familiar drive to their home that afternoon and rang the doorbell.

Jeff answered the door wearing jeans and a wrinkled t-shirt. His eyes were watering. I hugged him tight. "How's Kim taking this?"

"You know her. If there's a task that needs doing…"

Jeff had wrapped poor Blue in towels, but they couldn't disguise the labored breathing or the tremors in her short, fuzzy legs. She whined anxiously at my approach, and flinched away when I reached out to touch her.

"Take her and get it over with, Jeff," Kim ordered from her bed. "I can't stand seeing her like that another minute." For just a moment, her voice broke. "This isn't right. *I* was supposed to go first."

Before Jeff took Blue away, he lifted her up for a proper goodbye to Kim, and I stepped into the other room to allow them their privacy. Then he left with the dog, and it was just me and Kim.

"Oh, Kim," I said with tears in my eyes.

She managed to hold up a hand. "Stop it. Death is just a part of life. If you're going to stand there and cry at me, go away!"

I blinked the tears back and did my best to steady my voice. "What would you like me to do instead?"

"I want to talk about Vietnam today."

Kim normally didn't like to talk about her years as a nurse in-country, but that day, she told me many stories of soldiers and their horrific wounds. Not once did she cry. Not once did she mention Blue.

When I visited again the next week, Jeff pulled me aside. "I'm worried about Mom," he said. "I think she's developing dementia."

"*Kim?*" I couldn't think of a less likely candidate. "ALS isn't associated with cognitive decline, Jeff. Are you sure?"

"See for yourself."

I found Kim sitting in her wheelchair watching *M*A*S*H* on television. "If they showed it how it really was, all the viewers would puke," she told me.

I watched as she automatically reached down to pet Blue, then stopped herself. Now, surely, the breakdown would come. But it didn't. "Did Jeff tell you that stupid little dog of his ran away?"

What?

"Um, no, I hadn't heard that," I said. "Why don't you tell me about it?"

"Well, I was asleep when it happened, but I guess Jeff just opened the door and the little bitch ran out and disappeared. How's that for gratitude?"

Would Jeff have made up a story like that? But no, Kim had been there, had seen Blue on her last day. She was the one who had told Jeff to go and get it over with.

"Kim," I said, "Do you know who the President is?"

She knew. She also knew the date, the exact address where she lived, who she was, who I was, and that she was on hospice for ALS. "Are we through with the mental status exam?" she said sarcastically after she'd answered the last question.

I couldn't think of anything else to ask her. "What would you like to do today, Kim?"

"Let's watch the rest of this stupid program. If Jeff's father had looked like *that*," she said, as Alan Alda walked onscreen, "I would have married him."

My other visits with Kim were much the same. She either didn't mention Blue at all or said that Blue had run away when Jeff opened the door. It was an extreme form of denial, but Kim didn't seem any the worse for wear for it. The hospice staff and Jeff had a quick conference, and we decided that if it was more comforting for her to believe that Blue had run away, we wouldn't try to force her to accept the truth.

A month later, the hospice nurse who was managing Kim's care reported that Kim hadn't been out of bed in a week and that her lungs were very congested. Kim had declined antibiotics and didn't want to be put on a ventilator. "She's actively dying," the nurse said.

I went to visit Kim later that day. She was unresponsive. Jeff seemed at a loss, so I took one of Kim's hands, instructed Jeff to take the other, and asked him to share his favorite memories of Kim. "She liked to pretend she was a drill sergeant," he said, "but dig a little deeper and you'd find the sweetest woman in the world."

Kim's breathing began to change as we talked. Sometimes she panted for a few minutes and then she stopped breathing altogether for periods of ten seconds or more. I slipped outside to call the hospice nurse and tell her I thought Kim was going.

When I came back into the room, Kim was sitting straight up in bed. I couldn't believe my eyes. Kim hadn't sat up on her own in all the time I'd known her. She needed one or two people to support her and pillows to prop her up. But here she was, back erect, dark eyes searching. Her eyes flitted across Jeff's and across mine without a trace of recognition.

Then she looked down and to her right, at the area on her bed where Blue used to lie beside her when she was having a bad day. A beautiful smile blazed across her features, and her speech wasn't slurred at all as she said, "There you are!" Her hand stroked the empty mattress.

Then she slumped back in bed.

She was gone.

"What was that?" Jeff quavered, as tears started to run down his cheeks. "What the hell did we just see?"

I was crying, too. "I think we saw Blue come back for her."

"I don't believe in that. I thought you didn't, either."

"I don't," I said, and I didn't. But that moment with Kim made me wonder. Chemicals flooding a dying brain with soothing memories? Or a true visitation? Like I told Kim during our second meeting, I guess I'll have to wait until it's my turn to find out.

Chapter Five
The Great Fish Caper

Lily and Janet had shared a cozy, two-bedroom home in the suburbs for almost forty years, but their relationship went back much longer than that. They met while attending college to become teachers. They taught fifth-grade kids at different schools in the same city, each earning many Teacher of the Year awards and countless community medals along the way. Neither ever married nor had children. Although they were not of a generation comfortable with the terms "lesbian" or "gay," we all knew that only one of the bedrooms in the house was in use.

Lily was admitted to hospice shortly after Christmas. She had metastatic cancer from an unknown primary site, but luckily, she experienced little pain. Even though she was tired and short of breath, she insisted on giving us a guided tour of the home she shared with Janet, pointing out all the different Christmas decorations they had gathered over the years on their various trips. If there was an antique mall within twenty miles, Lily bragged, they could find it.

We ended the tour in Lily's bedroom where salt water fish glided through an aquarium that Lily had whimsically wrapped with green and red strings of Christmas lights. Presumably, the aquarium was located in the bedroom so Lily could enjoy the fish while she rested.

"Really," she confided to us in a conspiratorial whisper, "I'm not that fond of fish. Janet just wants them in here to protect them from Io and Oi."

Io and Oi turned out to be Lily's two Russian blue cats. They seemed fairly stoic about their banishment from the bedroom, claiming the couch and at least two kitchen counters as their own. Lily used to sit in a reclining chair in the living room and watch them with a sad, thoughtful smile.

As winter melted into the first thaw of the spring, however, Lily became bedbound. For the first time, I saw her argue with Janet. Either her cats were allowed to expand their territory into the bedroom or she, Lily, would spend the rest of her life on the couch. Her gray eyes blazed as she said it.

Janet backed down, but first she insisted on putting a fortress together to protect her fish. Lily and I watched, shaking our heads, as she constructed a solid wire cage to set over the aquarium. "Nice try, bums," she said, to the watching cats. "Looks like you're still confined to eating land animals."

Lily had what she needed to pass peacefully. She grew calm and restful and spent most of her days gazing at something in the upper left-hand corner of the room that only she could see. Janet, for her part, started looking more and more anxious. "I think some of my fish are missing," she confided in me as I was finishing up a visit.

I looked over at the aquarium and its wire armor. Nothing looked different to me. "Are you sure, Janet?"

"Yes!" she said indignantly. Then she lowered her eyes and rubbed her forehead. "No. I can't keep it straight anymore, what fish I have and don't have. Maybe I'm just imagining things."

"I'm not saying you're not right to be suspicious—cats and fish are long-time enemies, but I just don't see how…"

"Forget it!" Janet said sharply.

I waited a few minutes.

"I feel like I'm on a roller coaster," she said. "That damn cancer. We don't even know where it came from. All of a sudden it was just there, like a semi that skids right into your lane on an icy road, and all you can do is deal with it as best you can, try to get as few people killed as possible." Her eyes were full of pain. "I don't know how I'll go on living without her. Why her, Debra? Why not me?"

I squeezed her hand hard and didn't speak. Trying to answer her questions would only lead to platitudes that she didn't want to hear, and that I didn't want to say.

After a moment, Janet took a deep breath and pulled herself together. "It doesn't matter anyway, as long as Lily is happy," she said gruffly.

Lily was happy, but she was also off in her own little world. She slept more and seemed less aware of what was going on around her.

Even a hug and a kiss from Janet or an anxious purr from Io or Oi brought only a brief, befuddled smile to her lips.

"I'm losing her too soon!" Janet protested. "I knew the cancer would take her from me, but I didn't think she'd leave me while she was still alive."

The rest of the hospice team and I tried to explain to Janet that Lily's foggy state was a natural part of the body shutting down in preparation to die, but she was having none of it. "She could talk to me if she'd just focus," Janet said, glaring at the still figure on the bed. "I know she could."

One warm afternoon, about a week before Lily passed away, Janet needed to get out of the house to run some errands, see friends, and try to pull herself together. I volunteered to sit with Lily for a couple of hours. As Lily was barely conscious and no longer speaking, I took a stack of documentation I needed to complete. I made sure Lily was comfortable and didn't need anything, then settled into the chair beside her bed to catch up with paperwork. A couple of hours passed uneventfully.

Suddenly, I caught movement in my peripheral vision. Io and Oi strolled casually into the room. I assumed they had come for an afternoon nap with Lily, but instead they meandered towards Janet's aquarium.

I held my breath and watched as Io hooked the bottom of the cage with one paw, lifted it a few inches, and slithered under it. Oi followed suit.

I glanced at Lily, and found her gray eyes alert for the first time in days.

"You…you knew!" I accused her, laughing.

She held up a finger to her lips, and we both watched the rest of the performance unfold. Io leaped effortlessly to the top of the aquarium. I worried she might knock the whole thing over, but she was light and careful, and though the aquarium swayed a little, it didn't fall. Io stood watching the exotic fish for a minute. Then, quick as lightning, her paw flashed out, caught a fish, and tossed it out of the aquarium. She did this with all the panache of a diner at a five-star restaurant who has just selected his lobster for the main course.

Oi caught the fish in his mouth, and he and Io slithered under the wire cage and out of the room…past the sneakered feet of Janet, who had just returned from doing her errands.

Janet's face was beet red. "I'll be damned," she blustered. "Those psychopathic little bastards. I'm swear I'm going to make fur gloves out of them. I mean it! From now on, they are vegan cats!"

"Janet…" I put a restraining hand on her arm and nodded to Lily, who was still awake and giggling softly.

Janet's anger faded. Her eyes filled with tears as she walked towards the bed. She and Lily desperately needed this time together, and they needed to be undisturbed. I think I broke a world record sweeping all my half-finished papers into my arms and disappearing from the bedroom.

Later, a few months after Lily had passed peacefully while Janet held her hand, Janet told me that Lily had been fully present for about half an hour that day. They had talked, teased, reminisced, and spoken, possibly for the first time, of their great love for each other and their coming separation. Janet got to look directly into her partner's eyes and give voice to the significance of their lives together. It was as sacred and true as any marriage ceremony.

Janet said Lily disappeared back into her fog almost as quickly as she had appeared. Her face went slack and her eyes grew dull. She was once again lost in the world unique to those who are slowly dying.

But the things that needed to be said had been said, and the things that needed to be heard had been heard.

It's normal, as clients approach death, for them to show a last spark of energy. Sometimes they want to see family members or friends. Other times they want one last taste of a favorite meal. Occasionally, they want to go out for a drive, or sit in a special chair, or read from the Bible or another book that is meaningful to them.

Lily got her spurt of energy from the hijinks of two mischievous cats, and she used that very special time to honor a 60-year relationship that, until then, had dared not speak its name.

Chapter Six
The Birds

"I always thought he'd just die here, at the nursing home," Roy's wife, Ellen, told me in a hallway decorated by the artwork of the residents who lived in the care center. Behind us, the hospice nurse frowned as she spoke in fierce whispers into her cell phone, trying to make Roy's transfer home happen in time. "It's a nice place," Ellen continued, "and he gets good care here. But for the last two days he's been saying he wants to see Jasper and Jackie one more time."

"Who are Jasper and Jackie?" I asked.

Ellen looked at me as if I'd just asked the name of the President of the United States. "They're our Amazon parrots," she said "Our wedding gifts to each other."

As we spoke further, I learned that Roy and Ellen had been married ten years as of the previous month. It was a second marriage for both of them. They had much in common besides a love of birds. Both of their first marriages had ended with the deaths of their spouses. They also shared the same far left political ideals—in fact, they had met at a rally in support of a candidate for state senator. Roy was 61 then. Ellen was 57.

Their lives together had been a whirlwind of trips, activism, square dancing, caring for their beloved birds, and shamelessly spoiling the small grandchildren in their blended families. As busy as they were, no one thought much about it when Roy started to complain of feeling tired and out of sorts. Then one morning, he was simply too weak to get out of bed.

Medical tests showed a rare and aggressive form of leukemia. Roy underwent chemotherapy, but he was never able to achieve a remission. When it became clear that he was dying, he chose to go into a nursing home to spare Ellen the grief of watching him fade away at home. Now, however, the moment of death was close. Roy was panicky and wanted to return to their home and their birds.

Ellen wanted to honor his last wish. When the staff at the facility wasn't sure what to do, she called hospice to help oversee Roy's care and comfort.

I was a little dubious at first, because Roy was six feet tall and, in spite of his illness, weighed 200 pounds if he weighed an ounce, while Ellen, though a respectable 5'4", couldn't have weighed more than 125 pounds dripping wet.

Ellen immediately put my fears to rest. "I know what you're thinking," she said to the nurse and I. "You're wondering if I can manage him physically. I know just how much care he requires. But I'll have my children and his children to help me. We're a very close-knit family. I just don't want him to die upset and frightened. All he wants is to go home. Please help us."

I went into Roy's room to get the necessary paperwork signed.

He was alert and oriented but very weak. Keeping his eyes open was an effort, and when I handed him the pen, I might as well have been asking him to sign his name with a ten pound weight. "Roy," I said gently, "You made Ellen your power of attorney for health decisions when you first got sick. Do you remember that?"

He nodded.

"I think it would be easier on you if she signed the paperwork for hospice. Is that all right with you?"

He managed a weak grin. "Yeah. After ten years, I think I trust her." The smile faded and he clutched at my hand. "Do I get to go home?" he whispered, his grip on my fingers surprisingly strong. "Please tell me this means I get to go home. I don't want to die here."

"We'll get you home today, Roy," I promised. "We're having a hospital bed delivered to your house right now. As soon as that's all set up, we'll schedule an ambulance to take you home."

"Hurry!"

"We will, Roy. We're moving this along as fast as we can." But in the back of my mind, a warning bell went off. Roy clearly thought death was coming, and soon. I knew he would hang on as long as he could, but I just hoped we had time to get him home before his exhausted body gave out completely.

I went back out into the hall and told the hospice nurse and Ellen about my talk with Roy. "The medical equipment company just called to say the bed was set up," the nurse said as Ellen hurriedly scribbled her name on my paperwork. "Let's get that ambulance here right away."

Roy's blood pressure was starting to drop alarmingly by the time the ambulance arrived. I worried that even the simple act of moving him would cause his death, but he was stronger than I gave him credit for. The nurse and I trailed behind the ambulance in our cars. Ellen rode in the back of the ambulance with Roy, just in case. But the paramedic gave us a thumbs up as we pulled up outside Roy and Ellen's house fifteen minutes later. Roy had survived the trip.

I could hear the birds squawking and screeching noisily even before we entered the house. Inside, the living room was dominated by two massive bird cages. One cage held a bird that measured about 18 inches from beak to tail. He had green feathers and red and blue markings around his eyes. The other cage held an even larger bird with blue feathers. They rattled the bars of their cages, banged their toys around, and vocalized noisily to us and to each other, occasionally saying a rude word or two that Roy had evidently taught them.

Ellen turned the television on to one of Roy's favorite game shows and cranked up the volume so he could hear it even without his hearing aids.

I went to help the nurse get Roy settled and realized in dismay that the hospital bed had been set up between the two bird cages. Between Jasper, Jackie, and the television, I was afraid Roy would never find comfort. I'd only been there five minutes, and I already had a dull, pounding headache.

Jasper—or maybe it was Jackie—shrieked in my ear, and I winced.

Meanwhile, with the help of the nurse, Roy settled into his hospital bed and took a scheduled dose of pain medicine. "Roy, are you okay here?" I shouted over the chaos. "Would you rather we moved the bed into your bedroom?"

He didn't hear me. Instead he looked from one bird to the other and back again, as if he were trying to memorize their every feature. He stretched out his hand to touch the green bird's beak, and for just a second, the bird quieted down. The smile on Roy's face told me everything. It might be home sweet hell to me, but Roy was exactly where he belonged and where he wanted to be.

Less than half an hour later, as the nurse and I talked to Ellen, Roy's breathing changed. With the birds still chattering to either side of him and the television still blaring at the foot of the bed, he peacefully took a few last breaths and slipped away.

Roy might very well have died that same day at exactly the same time if we'd left him in the nursing home. Then again, he might have hung on miserably for weeks. We'll never know. But I am convinced of one thing.

Roy was a hundred times more contented and relaxed in that madhouse of a home than he would ever have been in the nicest nursing facility. Seeing his beloved birds again was what he needed to have a good death.

Chapter Seven

Fizzle

It took only one look at Barb to know she had lived a hard life. Her fifty-year old face was so deeply lined she looked more like a woman in her seventies. The thin, spider-web scars on her knuckles spoke to intimate experience with hand-to-hand combat. She chain smoked and cursed under her breath as she lay sideways across her hospital bed.

Barb seemed glad for the chance to share her life story. She spoke openly of her history of drug abuse, her years of being homeless, her devastating grief at the death of her only child in a car accident, and her rage at the cancer that was slowly stealing her life, "just when I was starting to get things together. How's that for a real kick in the goddamn balls?"

"Barb, honey, language," said her mother, a soft-spoken shadow of a woman who seemed to vanish into the walls during Barb's frequent rages.

"Jesus Christ, Mom, she's a social worker. She's heard it all before. Haven't you?" Barb demanded, turning to me.

I shrugged and nodded. If Barb had been another type of client, I might have said, "Surprise me," but I had the uneasy feeling that Barb would manage to do just that.

"*See?*" Barb scoffed at her mother.

"Just mind your manners, Barbie."

Barb looked like the kind of woman who would own a pit bull or a German shepherd. Instead, her companion of choice was a cloud-white teacup poodle named Fizzle.

Fizzle fit easily into the palm of Barb's broad hand. Although he had never been near a dog show, he was always immaculately groomed with an AKC show cut. Each time I visited, he had a different colored bow in his perfectly combed topknot.

Some French poodles are vocal dogs, yipping almost incessantly. Fizzle didn't bark—he bit. Anyone who tried to touch Barb, no matter how gently or lovingly, was likely to come away with Fizzle attached to her hand. I almost always give patients a hug or a handclasp at the end of each visit, but after a few encounters with Fizzle and his razor-sharp teeth, I learned it was wiser to wave goodbye to Barb when I was ready to go.

Barb was not an easy woman to care for. In fact, two hospices had already fired her for non-compliance with medication and for verbally abusing the staff. She was short-tempered, quick to complain, and slow to compliment. She took her medications when and if she felt like taking them and then cursed at the nurse because we couldn't get her symptoms under control. She threw me and her nurse out of the home more times than I can count, but we always came back, and she always accepted us with the sheepish air of a child who has just thrown a doozy of a temper tantrum.

After a few weeks, I noticed that Barb's mother had started to avoid the sickroom, leaving the lion's share of Barb's care to Barb's older sister.

That arrangement lasted about a month until Barb's sister left in a huff. Then an uncle came in to take care of her. She went through two or three more caregivers as her cancer slowly worsened. I got used to distressed relatives following me out of Barb's room so they could vent their own frustrations.

There wasn't a doubt in my mind that Barb's family was anticipating her passing with a sense of weary relief, so I was surprised when the hospice nurse called me on the day Barb died and asked me to come out to the home as quickly as I could.

I knocked on the front door and entered, prepared to be confronted by weeping, hysterical relatives, but Barb's sister met me in the hallway with a wry grin. "How are you?" I asked, giving her a hug.

"You know, we're all doing fine. We did our best for Barbie, and if you want the truth, she was lucky to live as long as she did. Mom's been afraid for the last thirty years that she was going to get a phone call that Barb had overdosed and died alone in some alley."

The nurse stuck her head out of Barb's room. "Boy, am I glad to see you!"

"What's wrong?" I asked. "Everyone seems to be doing fine."

"Not everyone." She gestured towards the bed.

I stepped into the room and heard a low growl. Fizzle was crouched on Barb's motionless chest. His teeth were bared, and he turned around in a slow circle as if defying anyone to make a move.

I summoned my most soothing voice and stepped towards him slowly. "Poor Fizzle. Poor little guy. You must be so confused. It's okay."

Fizzle waited until I was within range. Then he lunged at me and sank his teeth into the web of flesh between my thumb and index finger. I swore and jumped back. The bite had gone all the way through the flap of skin. I made a mental note to get a tetanus shot.

I noticed that several family members were also nursing bleeding wounds.

"Can somebody lend me a coat?" I asked, trying to sound braver than I felt. Someone thrust a jacket into my hands and I approached Fizzle again, using the material to shield my fingers. Fizzle didn't bother with my hands this time. He launched himself straight at my face. I batted him down, probably not as gently as I should have, and he returned to his spot on Barb's chest, never taking his eyes off me.

"This is ridiculous," I said, more to myself than to the family, "He's only about the size of a rat."

"But mean as a rattlesnake," Barb's sister said.

"I could shoot him," Barb's nephew offered.

"No one is shooting anything!" said Barb's mother.

"Maybe if we all go into the other room for a few minutes, he'll calm down," I said.

We traipsed into the living room and waited for about half an hour, not saying much. Then Barb's mother approached Fizzle again. He bit her on the wrist.

"*Now* can I get my gun?" the nephew asked.

"We have to do something," the nurse said. "I need to notify the funeral home to pick up the body. She can't just stay here."

She caught my eye, and I knew immediately what she was thinking. The house was warm, in spite of fans blowing in the windows, and decomposition can begin very quickly after death. I could already see a slight, suspicious swelling in Barb's abdomen.

"I'm calling animal control," I said finally. No one argued with me as I picked up the phone.

"The animal you're calling about is a teacup poodle?" the dispatcher asked me, disbelief stamping her voice. "Not a standard?"

"No, he's a teacup."

"And you said a *poodle*, right?"

"Yes," I said, feeling a little like snarling myself. "A poodle."

About an hour later, two men from animal control arrived. They entered the house laughing but sobered up quickly and murmured their condolences to the family when they saw Barb's body and realized what was going on. One of them made a half-hearted grab for Fizzle, and Fizzle delivered one of his trademark silent bites. The workers finally had to capture Fizzle with a control stick. The little poodle twisted and fought every inch of the way into the transfer cage.

"Please just take him away," Barb's mother said. "I can prove he's had all his shots, and I'll sign him over to anyone, but I can't manage him."

With Fizzle gone, we were finally able to summon the funeral home to pick up Barb's remains. The whole process had taken more than four hours.

I didn't think I'd ever hear about Fizzle again, but I followed the family for a year of bereavement, and after about six months, Barb's mother asked if I could find out what had become of the little dog. I told her gently that Fizzle had probably been euthanized. No animal shelter would take the risk of adopting out such an aggressive dog. She understood, but asked me to make the call anyway.

I found out that animal control had taken Fizzle to a shelter about ten miles away and gave the shelter a call, expecting to hear the worst. Instead, the woman on the other end of the line laughed when I described Fizzle. "You must mean my little guard dog," she said.

"Your...?"

"I was working the night they brought him in. I felt so sorry for the poor thing—we had to call the vet out to sedate him—so I decided to take him home to foster him. One thing led to another, and I've still got him. I can send you a picture, if you'd like."

"That would be great!" I said.

A few days later, the picture arrived in the mail. It showed Fizzle, white fur gleaming, red bow in his topknot, sitting on the lap of a woman who, like Barb, looked as if she hadn't lived an easy life.

I showed the picture to Barb's mother. She looked at it for a moment and a smile crossed her tired face. "Well, now, that's nice," she said. "I know some people live to come off of hospice, but I bet it's not every day you save a dog."

"No, I think it's a first for us," I agreed.

"I'm glad Fizzle got a second chance," she said. "It's just too bad that Barbie…"

I waited, but she didn't finish the thought. Instead she looked at the picture for another minute and quietly tucked it into the small pile of photos that represented the few happy times in Barb's life.

It was the last I ever saw of Fizzle.

Chapter Eight
Silence

"I'm going to my room so you and Larry can have a nice chat," Edwina said.

I managed a smile. I always dreaded my visits with Larry and Edwina. Larry was on hospice for end stage Alzheimer's disease. He hadn't been capable of having a "nice chat" since we admitted him. In fact, it had been months since I'd heard him say anything at all.

Edwina wasn't much of a talker either, but at least when she stayed in the room, I could usually strike up a conversation with her about her grandchildren. From Larry, I got absolutely nothing, not even a flicker of an eye.

Edwina didn't usually stay in the room when I visited, however. She took advantage of my time with Larry to claim some private time for herself. I certainly didn't blame her, but I hated being left alone with Larry and his geriatric golden retriever, Washington.

"Hi, Larry," I said, as the bedroom door shut softly but firmly behind Edwina. "How are you today?"

I probably would have fallen out of my chair if he had answered, but he didn't. Instead he silently fixed his big brown eyes upon me.

"The weather is great," I babbled on, "getting cooler every night now, and the leaves are starting to change colors…" I enthused about the autumn, the upcoming holidays, the November elections, and the football season for what felt like hours. When I checked my watch, however, only five minutes had gone by, and Larry's facial expression hadn't changed one bit.

In his corner basket, Washington had fallen asleep. I was a real hit with both of them.

I asked Larry about his days in the Air Force. Nothing.

I asked him if he remembered working in the coal mines of West Virginia as a young man. Nothing.

I had brought a children's book about the Presidents of the United States and read a few paragraphs about the men who had led the country when Larry was a teenager and a young adult. He still didn't respond, but I thought I caught a reproachful look, as if I should know better than to read to him from a picture book.

By the time I was finished reading, though, I had been there for about half an hour—long enough to end the visit. I tapped on Edwina's door to let her know I was going. She gave me a hug as she always did and said, "Thank you, dear, come again."

I crouched by Larry's chair and put my hand over his. "See you next time, Larry."

He showed no reaction, and I gave Washington a pat on the flank and hurried out, thankful that I had done my job for another two weeks.

My next visit went much the same as the one before it, except Washington came to stand beside the chair where I sat. He looked at his master with sad eyes.

By my visit after that, we'd had our first snow and the holidays were rapidly approaching. I sang Christmas carols to Larry. This time I didn't just imagine a reproachful look in his eyes. Washington hid in his basket. I drove away more frustrated than ever. Obviously, there was someone still very much at home inside Larry, someone who resented being condescended to. But damned if I knew how to reach that person.

I delayed my next visit for nearly three weeks. Christmas had come and gone, and I did a monologue about New Year's traditions and which football teams looked the most promising for the playoffs. As usual, Larry just looked at me.

I finally fell silent. I, who prided myself on being able to communicate with almost any dementia patient, was completely out of ideas. If Larry wanted quiet, well then, quiet he would get.

So we sat and looked at each other. Beneath the wrinkles and the blank stare, I could still see remnants of the handsome soldier who had grinned shyly at the camera on his wedding day and of the proud father holding aloft his first-born son. Did Larry still have access to any of those memories? I wondered. Or were they lost to him forever?

I opened my mouth to ask him, but changed my mind and let the silence continue. It wasn't really an uncomfortable stillness. In fact,

Larry seemed more relaxed than I had ever seen him. After a minute or two, Washington scrabbled out of his basket and walked over to stand between us.

And then, the miracle. I reached out my hand to pet Washington's golden coat, *and Larry did the same thing*. Our fingers touched, and I trembled with the intensity and longing I sensed in that groping, wrinkled hand.

Suddenly, Larry's face crinkled into a warm, happy smile. His brown eyes sparkled. I smiled back, but before my lips could complete their upward curve, the moment was gone. Larry's hand fell away from mine. His face and eyes were blank again.

Washington whimpered a little, and I stroked his head. "Never mind, boy," I whispered. "We know what happened, don't we?"

The connection had passed, but it had existed. Through Washington, Larry and I had shared a moment of absolute humanity that transcended illness and death.

I visited Larry and Edwina for another year, until Larry died quietly in his sleep. I did not connect with him so powerfully again, but I did learn to join him in his silent appraisal of the world. And every so often, when he reached out a shaking hand to pat Washington's beautiful golden fur, I knew there were traces of the old Larry still living in the shell that end-stage dementia had left behind.

Chapter Nine
The Wascally Wabbit

Most of our patients bond with animals because they love them so much. But as I learned one brisk November morning during an animal visit at a nursing home, there are other reasons to connect to furry creatures as well.

My client, Hal, was a feisty man in his eighties. Robbed of most of his speech by a stroke, he still managed to communicate with his clear blue eyes and a look of scorn that crossed his face when someone suggested something he felt was beneath his dignity. The few words he was able to summon indicated that his mind was very much intact.

The first time I met him, the activities director at the facility, a cheery, overly-enthusiastic woman had pushed Hal in his wheelchair to a group activity. They were, she explained in a booming voice, going to make little boats out of Popsicle sticks. I didn't need to know Hal to translate the look on his face to one of absolute horror.

The activities director went around passing out the Popsicle sticks. She stopped in front of Hal and crouched down by his wheelchair. "How would we like to make a boat today?" she asked.

Summoning every ounce of speech still left to him, Hal glared at her and said in a trembling, grating voice, "Now just why the fuck would *we* want to do that?"

Her face dropped, and I made my move. "Hi, I'm Debra, the hospice social worker. I need to take Hal back to his room to visit with him for a minute. Is that all right?"

It was more than all right with her.

Back in his room, Hal fixed me with a glare. He used one hand to hook the blanket that covered his legs and brought it up over his face so he wouldn't have to look at me.

I laughed. "Don't worry, I'm not going to ask you to do any crafts."

The blanket didn't move an inch.

"I would like to find out what you're interested in, though," I said. "You'll like it much more when I'm here if we can talk about something that really interests you. Are you a sports fan?"

For the next half hour, I tried to find something to engage him. I talked about the weather, politics—both liberal and conservative, the army, the textile industry which had been his life's work, pets, his children, his grandchildren, and even the food at the facility.

He kept the blanket over his head.

Fearing he might suffocate, I pulled it off. The look he gave me could have frozen boiling water. "It's okay," I said, "I'm going now. I just didn't want you to get too hot."

The next week, the blanket was back. I talked about activities at the facility that I thought might interest him, music, the holidays, his roommate, whether he would like a communication board to make it easier for him to express his wants. Nothing. The blanket stayed over his head. I felt like I was talking to a corpse.

By week three, I was getting desperate. I started telling him about myself, my pet cats, my love of Broadway musicals, my freelance writing career. "And of course," I said, "I love to read."

The blanket came down exactly three inches, revealing those intense blue eyes. "So do I," he rasped.

The stroke had robbed him of his ability to read, but he could still listen to stories and understand them. I got him hooked up with books on tape, and always brought along a book to read aloud to him when I came to see him. To my surprise, he favored the classics, especially anything by Jack London or Mark Twain. Before long, we found a volunteer who was willing to go out and read to him once a week, and he enjoyed that as well.

Once I knew what interested him, our relationship progressed rapidly. He even gave in and started using the communication board. We modified it to include phrases like, "Read that again," and "Skip that chapter, it's boring."

His behavior at the facility improved, too. Oh, he still glowered over tasks that he thought were silly, but he avoided the use of the F-bomb which sent the activities director into a frenzy. He could even be persuaded to help people with cognitive disabilities finish their little crafts.

We were all devastated when Hal had a second, more serious stroke and became paraplegic. The few words he had used in the past were gone, but he still seemed to enjoy our reading sessions, so anyone from hospice who visited him read aloud a few pages of his favorite books.

He seldom went to activities anymore, so I was surprised when I stopped by on one of my routine visits to find he wasn't in his room. I asked the nurse, and she directed me to the dining room where volunteers from a group called Pets for Life had brought in their animals for the residents to interact with. One woman had a fluffy black and white cat with blue eyes that reminded me a little of Hal's. It lay in her arms and purred and didn't seem to mind when some of the residents forgot and pulled at its soft fur. There was also a gentle black Labrador who was being petted by a few women who shared a table.

I spotted Hal immediately, sitting stoically in his wheelchair in the middle of it all. He made no effort to touch any of the animals, and his face had the familiar look of scorn. I was about to rescue him, when he laid eyes on the rabbit.

It was a large, white, lop-eared rabbit cradled in the arms of a volunteer. He grunted and sat up so straight his wheelchair jerked. The nurse and I ran to steady it at the same moment. I beckoned the volunteer over.

"Do you like the rabbit, Hal?" I asked, surprised. I had figured he would go for one of the dogs.

Hal strained in his seat again and attempted to speak. His eyes were shining.

The volunteer held the rabbit out to him, but he didn't touch it. Again, he blurted a few words I couldn't understand.

The nurse, however, suddenly turned and ran from the room with her hand over her mouth. I made sure the brakes on Hal's chair were locked and followed her. She had retreated into an empty room and was bent over at the waist from laughing so hard.

"Honestly," I said, "what is so funny? I think it's sweet that he likes the rabbit."

That produced another mad gale of laughter.

It was two or three minutes before she calmed down enough to explain. "Didn't you hear what he was saying?"

"No," I confessed, "I haven't been able to understand him since that second stroke."

She giggled again. "He was saying, 'Get me my gun.' He didn't want to *pet* the rabbit. He wanted to *hunt* it!"

I couldn't help it. I started laughing, too.

"Oh, God," the nurse said, "how are we going to tell that poor volunteer?"

"We're not," I said, trying to pull myself together. "Let her think that rabbit was just what he needed to make him feel better. In an odd kind of way, I guess it was. But let's get back out there before he decides to wring its neck or something"

By the time we reached the dining room, Hal had decided there was no gun forthcoming and lost interest in the rabbit. When I took him back to his room, though, he was still talking excitedly and from the few words I caught, I gathered he was telling me about hunting trips he had taken with his sons.

The next time I visited Hal, I brought some hunting magazines I had borrowed from friends. He stared wistfully at the pictures as I read him the stories, stories that made my stomach churn but that he, obviously, loved.

Hal didn't live long after the rabbit incident. A third stroke robbed him of his sight, and soon after, a fourth put him into a comatose state. He died comfortably a few days later.

At the funeral, his eldest son asked the hospice staff who had cared for him to slip something meaningful into his casket. The staff and I thought about it, and after careful consideration, we buried him with a copy of *Call of the Wild*, his favorite Jack London book…and with a stuffed white rabbit.

Chapter Ten

Get Me a Knife

I can remember only one other case where a profound dislike of a pet actually produced therapeutic results.

I was sitting cross-legged on the floor beside Janeen's chair. We were signing Janeen on to hospice for advanced Parkinson's disease. Janeen had the look of one who was completely and utterly exhausted. She asked her daughter, Rose, to sign the necessary paperwork. When she had to answer a question, she did so in a reed-thin voice with no volume behind it. Even sitting as close as I was, I often had to ask her to repeat herself. This invariably earned me a reproachful look and a tired sigh.

I put my hand on the floor to push myself closer to Janeen's chair...

...and a long, furry creature came flying out from under the sofa, skimmed up my arm, and settled itself on my shoulder.

I shrieked and jumped to my feet. "What the--?"

Rose looked at me as if I'd sprung an antenna. "That's Wren. He's a ferret."

Wren, who had not been at all abashed by my scream and subsequent leap, wound himself around my neck like a scarf. He was actually pretty cute, with black, beady eyes that seemed to reflect a sense of humor and soft brown fur that gave way to a patch of white on his belly. Cute or not, though, I wasn't quite ready to kiss and make up. My heart was still pounding.

"I don't believe animals belong in cages," Rose said cheerfully.

"I can see that," I said, giving her what I hoped was a withering look. "So what other…wildlife…am I likely to encounter?" If there was a python slinking around waiting to give me a hug, I wanted to know it.

Rose thought for a moment. Just the dogs. And Dusty, the cat. We did have some white rats running around here, but I haven't seen them in weeks. They must have got outside. And then there's Wren. That's it."

I smiled sourly and turned back to Janeen as the ferret settled itself more comfortably around my neck.

All of a sudden, Janeen leaned forward and clutched at my hand with more strength than I would have expected from her. She said clearly, "Get…me…a…knife!"

"Mom!" Rose reproved her. "Mom's not a big fan of Wren's," she added to me.

If Wren had done that little run, jump, and climb trick on Janeen, I could certainly understand why.

Once I got used to all the animals, my next few visits to Janeen were pretty uneventful. She now sat in a special wheelchair instead of her recliner, and her speech grew even softer and more slurred. She slept most of the time.

Still, whenever Wren made one of his unexpected appearances, her words were strong and audible. "Get…me…a…knife."

I suggested to Rose that it might be a good idea to keep Wren and Janeen separated.

"Oh, it's all right," Rose said. "Mom couldn't really hurt him."

"I'm not so worried about Wren," I said, "It's Janeen I'm thinking about. Wren seems to upset her."

"Animals are therapeutic," Rose insisted.

"Well, yes, normally that's true," I agreed. "But Wren really startles Janeen when he darts out of nowhere and runs up her body. And remember, she doesn't even have the coordination to pick him up and put him back on the floor like you and I do."

"Gosh," said Rose, without much concern. "I hadn't thought about it like that." But she did nothing to change the situation, and Janeen continued to be a victim of Wren's sometimes violent affections.

Janeen's condition deteriorated more quickly than any of us had anticipated. Within a month after hospice admission, she had stopped eating and was completely confined to bed. The hospice nurse and I both tried to tell Rose that Janeen's prognosis was poor, but Rose brushed us off. "I'm not worried. Mom's tough. She'll live another ten years."

I was not surprised when the hospice nurse told me that Janeen had entered the active dying phase. I went out to the house. Janeen lay on the hospital bed we had gotten for her. Her eyes were half closed, and her breath rattled in her chest.

"What's happening?" shouted Rose.

"I think we're getting very close to the end," the nurse told her, as Janeen's breathing changed.

"Nooooo!" Rose howled. She fell on her knees by Janeen's bed and clasped her mother's hand. "Please, Mom, don't do this to me. Not yet. I'm not ready. Please!"

The nurse and I exchanged looks, uncomfortably aware that each breath could be Janeen's last.

Then it happened. A pink nose appeared over the edge of the mattress. Wren had scaled the bed clothes and was dashing across the bed towards Janeen. I made a grab for him, but he slipped through my fingers and scrambled up Janeen's laboring body. His little claws left red tracks on her arm.

Janeen screeched, suddenly completely alert. She slapped at Wren, but he was much too fast for her. Color rose in her face, and the familiar words roared from her throat: "Get…me…a…knife!"

Wren might have scared the living crap out of Janeen, but he also pulled her back from the brink of death. Her breathing remained steady for the rest of the afternoon, and she remained conscious as her watchful eyes darted back and forth. Two days later, she was accepting small bites of food. The next week, she was back in her wheelchair. She survived for another three months.

Rose and the hospice nurse and I had a lot of long talks during those weeks, and when the time finally came for Janeen to go—for real—Rose was able to plant a kiss on her mother's forehead and whisper, "Go with God, Mom."

A few weeks later, I visited Rose for bereavement. As soon as I sat down, Wren scrambled up my leg and into my lap. Rose snickered. "Remember the first night you all were out here, and Wren climbed up your arm?"

I, too, laughed at the memory.

Rose waved her finger in my face. "And I was right all along. He did turn out to be therapeutic. He kept Mom here until I understood what was happening and was ready to let her go."

I stroked the ferret curled up on my legs and thought about all the things I could say. In the end, I opted for silence. This, I decided, was definitely a case of all's well that ends well.

Chapter Eleven
It's Time to Say Goodbye

As I sat on a wooden chair in the small but cozy farmhouse, it occurred to me that I had never met a more unlikely pair of farmers. New York born and bred, Glenn and Alex sat together on a green couch with gray stuffing oozing out of one corner. Alex kept a protective arm wrapped around Glenn's shoulders as they answered my questions in flat voices with heavy Brooklyn accents.

Alex projected a hint of menace, Glenn, of exhaustion and defeat. Glenn was emaciated from the ravages of HIV. Although Alex had wrapped a down quilt around him, Glenn still shivered slightly as he spoke.

Cold…or nervous? I couldn't tell for sure, and I certainly couldn't ask with Alex's dark brown eyes warning me off. I wished I could find words to put the both of them at ease.

The answer presented itself in the form of a brown, long-haired creature with a body the size of a guinea pig, ears like a gremlin, protuberant eyes and three-inch log spindly legs. The long-haired Chihuahua—for that was what it was—launched itself towards the couch. Alex caught it in mid-air and set it on Glenn's lap. The Chihuahua yawned, walked a couple of circles around Glenn's knees, and settled in for a nap.

"That's Frankie," Glenn said. "We can put him in the other room if he bothers you…"

"Or we could find a social worker who isn't bothered by him," Alex added.

I hastened to reassure both men that I found Frankie adorable and that I was glad they had his loving companionship.

"He's a throw-away," Alex said roughly. "Like us."

"Al…" Glenn said mildly. I noticed his shaking had increased.

"No, damnit, she thinks she wants our life story. Let's see if she can handle it."

It was a story I'd heard far too many times, and it never failed to break my heart. Glenn and Alex had both been kicked out of their respective homes by their parents when they were in their early teens. Their only crime was being gay.

With no family support and no Fortune 500 companies hiring gay 13-year-olds, the two survived the only way they could—on the streets. This meant stealing from tourists and grocery stores, sleeping wherever they could find a secure place, and, often, selling their bodies to make ends meet. Alex's face was expressionless as he talked about being raped, stalked by gay-bashers, and tormented by policemen, but I thought I saw a tear in Glenn's eye.

Alex and Glenn had met at a youth homeless shelter when they were both fifteen. They had been inseparable ever since. On nights when the soup kitchens were empty, the shelters filled to capacity, and the tricks rough and cruel, they clung to each other in alleys and dreamed of the lives they would one day lead.

Glenn's great grandfather had been a farmer. Glenn decided he and Alex would own a small farm, somewhere far, far away from New York City. Nothing fancy—some crops, a few chickens, maybe a cow or two.

They started saving every cent they made and spent hours in the library learning what they could about farming. As soon as they were both 18, they moved to the Midwest and studied agriculture in a community college. They got a cheap apartment, took two or three jobs at a time, and watched their savings grow.

A few years later, Glenn heard about an older, childless couple who needed to sell their small family farm so they could move to long-term care. He and Alex made an offer on the farm, it was accepted…and just like that, their dream had come true.

The day after they moved into the farmhouse, they were sitting at the kitchen table having a breakfast of eggs laid by their very own hens when they heard a frightened little "whoop." They ran outside and found a disheveled Chihuahua puppy limping down the gravel road to their farm. Somehow, the puppy's paw had gotten caught in a mousetrap. That could have been accidental. But the cuts, bruises, and cigarette burns on his tiny body had been deliberately inflicted.

The two men didn't even need to speak to decide what to do. They would not turn their faces away from a fellow outcast. They spent weeks nursing Frankie back to health and even longer teaching him not to fear a man's voice or touch. By the time I came along, almost a year later, their efforts had succeeded beyond their wildest imaginings. Frankie was more than just a pet. He was a friend and a good luck talisman.

Running the farm was hard work. Not sure how folks in the rural area would react to the presence of two gay men, Glenn and Alex did everything they could by themselves. Some days they slept only a few hours; others, they were up round the clock. Neither one of them thought much of it when Glenn, who almost never wore a coat or a jacket, started to develop a series of upper respiratory infections.

The next few months flew by. To their surprise and delight, the farm prospered, but Glenn's health grew steadily worse. When he collapsed trying to walk across the kitchen, Alex dragged him to a local hospital.

The doctors did tests all day. In the evening, a kindly, white-haired man came in to ask them about their sexual histories. He then told them, sadly, that sometime during his years on the streets, Glenn had been exposed to HIV and now had AIDS. Alex, somehow, had escaped unscathed.

The hospital sent Glenn home on medication, but it made him sick, and it didn't stop the slow, steady destruction of his immune system. His weight dropped alarmingly, and his infections came more frequently and were more difficult to treat. Alex was going crazy trying to run the farm by himself and handle Glenn's medical needs as well. Finally, the doctor who had been so kind to them that first night suggested that it was time to involve hospice.

Alex cursed the doctor and stormed out of the office. "I'll never give up on you," he told Glenn now. "Never!"

Glenn, who was becoming more tired and withdrawn, took a different view. "It's not giving up…it's like looking for help somewhere else. If hospice can help me and if they can help you, I say we try it." He petted Frankie who had curled up in a ball on his stomach.

Alex finally gave in, but he wasn't happy about it. What if the hospice workers were disrespectful to him and Glenn? What if they thought he wasn't doing a good enough job providing care and took Glenn away from him?

It took me several visits and several hours of listening quietly before Alex came to accept that hospice really was there to help him and Glenn, not to trick or abuse them.

In spite of their rough beginnings, Alex and Glenn were proud of the relationship they'd made work against all odds. They loved to tell stories about fun times they'd shared and fun things they'd done.

As they talked to me, little Frankie would invariably back up until his hind legs touched the far wall. Then he would dash at the couch and leap as high as he could, which wasn't nearly high enough. Without missing a word in whatever he was saying, Alex would catch him in mid-air and transfer him to Glenn's eagerly-waiting hands.

Glenn continued to lose strength, suffering one devastating infection after another. By the middle of November, he could no longer get out of the hospital bed that hospice had provided. He used oxygen most of the time, too. Alex and I took turns going to the library and finding him books and DVDs on agriculture. At first Glenn was interested, but eventually his eyes took on a dreamy look, almost as if he were gazing at something through the ceiling.

"Do you think Glenn will live until Christmas?" Alex asked me one day.

It was the fourth of December. Already, the ground was dusted with light snow flurries. Glenn had stopped eating except for a few bites of broth here and there. Alex could get him to drink about a cup of water a day, when Glenn was awake, but he was rarely awake.

"I don't know," I admitted. "He's declining very fast. If you want Christmas with him, I think you should have it now."

"You mean…trick him?" for just a second the old anger flared in Alex's eyes. "I wouldn't do that. It wouldn't be fair."

"Why not? It's not like you're playing a joke on him to be mean. You've giving him a last Christmas with you. Isn't that really all that matters?"

Frankie whined around Alex's feet, and Alex picked him up. "I'll think about it."

Alex and Glenn celebrated Christmas on the second Saturday in December. Alex cut down a huge tree and strung it with lights of every color and decorations Glenn had picked out during a rare car trip to Wal-Mart. They lit their fireplace. Matt gave Glenn a little stuffed Chihuahua and the last book in the Harry Potter series. Best of all, Glenn actually ate a slice of turkey and a spoonful of mashed potatoes, and the food stayed down.

Frankie took part in the celebration as well. He pranced around wearing a headband with antlers bigger than he was and a Christmas bell on his collar that drove him crazy by ringing every time he moved. When Glenn and Alex started singing Christmas carols, Frankie even chimed in with a howl or two, though we decided he was probably protesting the bells and the antlers rather than showing true holiday spirit.

They both said it was a perfect day.

After that, Glenn seemed to let go entirely. His eyes, wide and full of wonder, followed things on the ceiling that we couldn't see. He never spoke to hospice staff anymore, and only rarely had a word for Alex or Frankie.

Alex was relieved that Glenn was in no pain, but he mourned their lost connection. He also worried that he would not be present when Glenn died.

"We've been there for each other for nearly twenty years," he told me tearfully. "I remember one time I picked up the wrong guy and got the crap beat out of me. Glenn couldn't take me to a hospital—I'd have wound up in foster care—so he sat up with me for 36 hours until I started to come around. I can't abandon him while he's dying." He absently caught Frankie in mid-leap and transferred him over to Glenn's bed.

The hospice nurse and I tried to explain that no one could predict the exact moment of Glenn's death, so there was no way to guarantee that Alex would be there. "I think he'll die very easily," I told Alex. "He'll just slip away. It won't be traumatic or scary. You've kept your promise to him, Alex. You've been with him through the worst part of this horrible disease. That's when he really needed you, and you were there."

Alex nodded. He took every precaution, though. He sat up with Glenn for days on end, and, when he could no longer keep his eyes open, he grabbed a couple of restless hours of sleep on that torn green couch.

After about a week of this, a nurse pulled me to one side when I got into the office in the morning and told me that Glenn had died during the night. I called Alex, who asked if I could come over right away.

We hugged in the doorway of the familiar farmhouse, trying not to see the blank space where Glenn's hospital bed should have been. I was afraid to ask him if he had been present when Glenn died. Instead I scooped up Frankie and stroked his silky fur.

Alex spoke first. His nose was red, and dried tears stained his cheeks, but his eyes were as calm as I'd ever seen them. "I have just had the most amazing experience of my life," he whispered.

"Can you tell me about it?" I whispered back, somehow knowing the silence was sacred.

"I knew last night that I'd had it," Alex said. "I was through. There was no way I could stay awake for another night, so I went to Glenn, took his hand, and said, 'I'm sorry, honey. I'm just so sorry.' And he just gave me that dreamy look, you know, like he had no idea what I was saying.

"I wanted to try to break through to him, but I was so damn tired all I could do was collapse on the couch. I fell asleep like this." He snapped his fingers.

"Later, I don't know how much later, I felt this solid *thump* on my chest. I woke up right away, and there was Frankie, standing on top of me. I couldn't believe he'd gotten up there all by himself.

"Anyway, he started barking in my face. I tried to push him off me, but he wouldn't budge, and he just kept barking louder and louder.

"I was really getting pissed, so I sat up and put Frankie on the floor. And he raced over to Glenn's bed.

"I followed him. The minute I touched Glenn's hand, Frankie shut up. Glenn's hand was warm but his breathing was…different…labored, I guess. Have you ever seen that before?"

I nodded silently and put the struggling Frankie back on the floor.

"Then Glenn took this really deep breath, and his chest stopped moving. I screamed, 'Breathe, baby, oh please, breathe!' or something stupid like that. And he did breathe. Just one more time. Then it was over."

Despite the tears, the look on Alex's face was one of total peace.

Frankie whined. He was scrabbling with his little paws to get purchase to jump onto the couch beside us. Alex reached down to help him up.

"Why did you have to help Frankie up just now?" I asked. "You said he jumped on your chest last night…"

"I know. He did," Alex said. "But he's never done it before, and he hasn't been able to do it since." He thought for a moment. "Waking me up so I could say goodbye to Glenn. That's a pretty damn special Christmas present, wouldn't you way?"

I swallowed but couldn't seem to get past a lump in my throat. "Sounds like a good present to me."

I had expected Alex to return to New York after Glenn's death. After all, the farm had been Glenn's idea. But Alex stayed, and he made good. Anybody who drives up that gravel road today will immediately be treated to the sight of a dozen cats and dogs in all states of health—throwaways, as Alex once described himself. Alex loves them all.

But his true adoration is reserved for Frankie, the little Chihuahua who loved him so much that he let him know when it was time to say goodbye.

Chapter Twelve

We Don't Allow Animals in the House

"Do you have any pets?" I asked. My eyes traveled from Jack, lying in his hospital bed in the middle of the living room and looking like he wished he could just disappear, to Louisa, standing stiffly behind the bed. Her hand rested the headboard, but she made no move to extend her arm an extra few inches to touch Jack's shoulder.

Jack answered me with a wry smile, a roll of his eyes to indicate the immaculate room, and a shake of the head.

"We don't believe animals belong in the house, dear," Louisa explained, looking pointedly at the fur covering my sweater.

My face grew hot, and I bit back the urge to explain that my youngest cat had slipped into my closet and slept on my fresh laundry the night before. Instead, I just went on to the next question.

I soon learned that Jack, and especially Louisa, didn't tolerate any kind of mess or disorder. The next time I visited their home, Louisa met me in the doorway and handed me a roll of tape to remove any stray cat fur from my clothes. I went through two sheets before she finally decided I was clean enough to come in. "I don't even know where that came from," I tried to explain. "Normally the cats don't get near my clothes."

"Fur tends to get everywhere when you open your home to furry creatures," Louisa said.

I felt the overwhelming urge to stick my tongue out at her while her back was turned, but I suppressed it. *Professional,* I reminded myself. *You're a professional.*

If things were rough for me in that house, they were doubly hard for Jack. He was humiliated that his advancing stomach cancer caused him to vomit frequently and to lose control of his bowels and bladder. Even though Louisa expressed willingness—albeit grudging willingness—to care for him, Jack insisted on hiring a private duty nurse's aide, Clarice, to help him stay as clean and odor free as possible.

Clarice, a large black woman with a loud laugh and a motherly manner, hit it off with Jack immediately, but she was soon at odds with Louisa about the occasional dirty shoe print on the white carpet or a plate that made it into the dishwasher without being rinsed quite thoroughly enough.

Clarice pulled me aside one day. She was furious, "If it wasn't for that poor man in the bed, I'd walk out the door and never come back," she said. "That Louisa—she's not a woman, she's a devil. I don't think she gives a damn if Jack dies as long as he keeps her house clean while he's doing it."

I tried to explain to Clarice that people exhibit grief in many ways and that perhaps claiming control of the environment was Louisa's. Clarice snorted and returned to Jack.

Next, I caught Louisa alone and tactfully mentioned that she would be doing a great service to her husband if she could find a way to make peace with Clarice for the next few weeks.

Louisa's eyes filled with tears. "I expect you think I'm just a fussy old woman."

"N...noooo," I said carefully. "It's your house and you have the right to set standards about how you want it kept. It's just that I know Jack is more important to you than a carpet which can be easily cleaned."

"I remember the Great Depression," Louisa said, wrapping her arms around herself as if to hold back the memories. "My family and I lived in a shanty with a dirt floor. Rats and insects were our roommates. They came in through the door and the windows and sometimes from under the ground. They wanted our food, and we had little enough as it was..." She shuddered.

"I was barely seven years old at the time, but I promised I would never, ever live like that again. And I never have."

My heart contracted as I tried to picture a seven-year-old with Louisa's gray eyes battling a rat for her breakfast. "You've made a beautiful home here," I told her softly. "I can understand why you want to keep it that way. Can I tell Clarice what we have talked about? It may help her to understand why cleanliness is so important to you."

Louisa nodded briefly.

I had a conversation with Clarice, and from then on we tried to be especially careful to respect Louisa's need for neatness and order.

As expected, Jack's decline was rapid. Within two weeks, he was refusing food and water. A couple of days after that, he slipped into a semi-comatose state that only Louisa's voice could penetrate. Even though he clutched at the bed covers as if he were cold, he began to perspire profusely. Everyone who worked with him kept a cool, damp washcloth on hand to bathe his face and hands.

One morning, during a routine visit, I went over to Jack to wipe the perspiration from his brow. His eyes were partially open, unseeing. When I touched his forehead with the washcloth, he uttered a contented sigh, pressed his cheek against my hand, and died.

Louisa said very little while we waited for the hospice nurse to arrive to confirm that death had occurred and, after that, while we waited for the funeral home to come pick up Jack's remains. She pulled a chair to the bed very close to her husband but did not make any attempt to touch his body. I offered her a glass of water and a warm sweater to wrap around her shoulders. She acted as if she didn't hear me.

I got the message, shut my mouth, and sad down next to her to wait. Every so often, a tiny shiver worked its way through her body.

After the funeral home came to remove Jack, Louisa stirred a little. "I've always thought that bed looked horrible in the middle of the room. Do you think…?"

"It will be gone by the end of the day," the nurse promised.

Louisa's shoulders relaxed a little.

During the next month, Louisa called me twice and asked in a panicky voice if I would come over to talk to her. Each time, she wanted reassurance that Jack's pain had been controlled when he died and that he hadn't "embarrassed himself."

I listened to her fears and reminded her of the powerful medications we had used to keep Jack comfortable. I also assured her that he left this world like the gentleman he was.

Those things seemed to be all she needed to hear. My visits never lasted longer than 20 minutes.

Then a month went by, and I realized I hadn't heard a word from Louisa. Concerned, I called her. She seemed both pleased to hear my voice and a little nervous.

"Oh, yes, by all means, come out to see me," she fluttered. "I just hope…well, we've been through so much together, I just don't want you to think badly of me."

I wondered what she could have done that would make me think badly of her. Was she involved in another relationship? Louisa hadn't seemed the type to rebound so quickly, but it could happen.

"Louisa," I said, "I would never judge you. I'll be there in half an hour."

The house looked the same when I pulled up the driveway. The grass was chemically green and cut with a barber-like precision. Not a twig in the shrubbery appeared as much as a millimeter out of place.

I rang the doorbell.

Louisa answered the door, blushing as if I'd caught her in the middle of a tryst. Her invitation to come in was a little hesitant, but I was curious, so I stepped boldly into the house.

Then, I saw it. Sitting in the middle of that pristine white rug was a small gray and white tabby cat. It was poised so perfectly with its tail wrapped around its body that I thought it was a statue. Then it meowed and walked over to rub its head against Louisa's legs, leaving a few stray hairs on her tailored pants.

Louisa's face had turned a dull red that went all the way to her hairline. She could not have been more embarrassed if I *had* caught her with another man, but she reached down to stroke the cat's ears.

I waited, sensing any questions would just make things more difficult for her.

She indicated for me to take a seat in the living room and poured me a cup of sweet, hot tea. Then she sat down opposite me. The little cat jumped into her lap, and she made no move to dislodge it. In fact, she rubbed its head. She still hadn't made full eye contact with me.

"It isn't mine," she said finally.

I waited.

"My youngest son got this cat for his teenage daughter. Two weeks ago he found out he and his family were being transferred into Hawaii. Do you know how hard it is to get a cat into Hawaii?"

I nodded sympathetically.

"So I said I'd take it. For a few days. Until he could find someone else."

"I see."

"She doesn't shed much. If I vacuum a little more often, no one even notices the fur."

"That's good."

"She cried the first night she was here, so I picked her up and put her on the foot of my bed. She sleeps on my pillow now."

I couldn't resist a smile. "They do tend to migrate. Give them an inch…"

"I feel terrible when I think of all the trouble I gave you about your clothes having cat fur on them. You must think I'm such a hypocrite."

"That's all water under the bridge. Besides, you're entitled to change your mind. What's her name?"

"Tabitha," Louisa said proudly. "I call her Tabby or Tabs for short. Just don't expect to see her the next time you come visit. I'm sure my son will have found her a better place to stay by then."

But Tabby was still there on my next visit to Louisa, and on my next. By the third visit, Louisa had stopped referring to Tabitha as her son's cat and talked proudly about how smart "her" cat was and all the tricks she had learned.

One day, as we sat drinking tea and watching Tabitha chase sunbeams on the carpet, Louisa said, very quietly, "I wouldn't have let on at the time, but when Jack died, I wanted to go, too. I just didn't see anything else good coming out of life."

Tabitha raced for a shadow, stopped too fast, and turned a somersault. Louisa and I both hid our smiles to preserve the cat's dignity.

"Sometimes even when you think you've lost all that you could possibly lose, there are still good things waiting for you," I suggested.

Louisa shrugged. "I suppose. But who'd have thought one of those things would come in the form of a cat?"

Chapter Thirteen
The Man Who Loved Horses

Gus was a lanky 72 year old man with brain cancer. He came on hospice after suffering a stroke. The first time I met him, he was in his private room at a local nursing facility. He was scrunched into a bed that could scarcely contain his 6'4" frame. The bed was placed next to the window, but the drapes were drawn. Propped up against three firm pillows, Gus was furtively chewing tobacco. He almost swallowed it when I knocked on his door. Then, when he saw I wasn't a nursing home employee, he spat the tobacco into a white Styrofoam cup and gave me a big grin.

"Thought you were the Gestapo," he said. "They don't like me chewing in here."

I looked at the brown stains on the floor and could understand why.

"Don't tell on me," he said with a wink, and put another pinch of tobacco in his cheek.

Gus was a born storyteller. That first day, he regaled me with tales about the small farm he and his wife had owned. I heard about their children, their fainting goat, the mean rooster who chased everyone until his then 12-year old daughter bashed it with a school book, and their very first cow. He and his wife had named the cow Sirloin to remind themselves that the cow was not a pet—she would be going to market, and soon. She ended up dying of old age on the farm.

Gus was still laughing about Sirloin when I asked, "How about horses? Did you have any of those?"

The smile faded from his face as if someone had dimmed a light switch. His green eyes grew moist, and he looked away from me. "Sure," he said, "we had horses. Can we talk another time? I'm getting a little tired now."

I left, but Gus' reaction to my question stayed in my mind over the next couple of days. I finally called his oldest son, Roger, who turned out to be every bit as friendly and talkative as his father.

"I'm not surprised Pop clammed up when you asked about horses," Roger said. "After Mom died, the only thing that kept him going was his bay gelding, Lightning. Sometimes he used to sleep in the stables, just to be near him. The only thing he really hated about having to go to the nursing home was leaving Lightning behind. It's still a big sore spot."

"What happened to Lightning after your dad went to the nursing home?" I asked.

"Oh, he's still on the farm," Roger said. "My wife and I moved out here after Mom died, and we'll keep the place going as long as any of the animals are left alive. That's what Pop wanted."

"Do you think Gus would like a picture of Lightning?"

"I brought one to the nursing home right after he moved there," Roger said, "but he turned away. He said it made him too sad to look at it."

My heart went out to Gus. I tried to imagine how lonely I'd be if I had to go to a nursing home and leave my cats behind.

The nursing home where Gus lived was close to our office, so I tried to check in on him whenever I had a few spare moments. He thrived on the extra attention, and he always sent me away laughing.

As his cancer progressed, he became weaker and more tired, but he never lost his sense of humor. Much to the irritation of the housekeeping staff, he also never lost his fondness for chewing tobacco, either. He even talked me into replenishing his supply a time or two.

As close as Gus and I became, though, he never once mentioned Lightning, and I never brought the subject up either. I thought it was one of those issues that would, sadly, go unresolved until his death.

Roger called me during the first week in August. "I just spoke to the hospice nurse," he said. "She says Pop is failing. She doesn't think he'll last much longer."

The nurse and I had spoken just that morning, and she had told me the same thing.

"His birthday is August 28," said Roger. "Do you think he'll live to celebrate it?"

"I hope so," I said, "but I'm afraid there aren't any guarantees."

"Damn," said Roger. "My brothers and sisters are coming in from out of town. We were all planning to surprise Pop with a party."

"Do you think they could come any sooner?" I asked.

Roger was silent for a moment. Then he said, "I'll make it happen by the end of the week."

Two days later, he called me back. "Everyone will be here on Friday," he said. "Pop doesn't suspect a thing. We'd love it if everyone on his hospice team could come to the nursing home and celebrate with us."

I promised to pass the word along.

The next day, Roger called me again. "I've just had the craziest idea," he said. "Do you think the facility would let me bring Lightning in a horse trailer? I could walk him around to Pop's window so Pop could see him."

I felt tears sting my eyes. "I can't imagine a birthday present he'd love more," I said. "Let me see if I can work things out with the facility."

Working things out with the facility proved remarkably easy. The staff there loved Gus every bit as much as the hospice team did, even if he did spit like a grasshopper. The administrator not only agreed to allow the horse trailer in the parking lot, he suggested having their maintenance man remove the screen on Gus' window so that Gus could actually touch his horse.

I called Roger back with the news.

That Friday, we all descended upon Gus' room: the hospice nurse, chaplain, aide, and I; all of Gus' children and grandchildren; and everyone who cared for him at the facility. Gus had gotten too weak to sit up in bed, but his grin still held all of its old sparkle as he looked from face to face. "You're all here," he said, over and over. "I can't believe you're all here."

His grandchildren helped him open his birthday cards and a few brightly-wrapped presents, and we all sang, "Happy Birthday." Gus was having too much trouble swallowing to tolerate any cake or ice cream, but he assured us he didn't care for sweets anyway. The facility nurse even let him chew his tobacco, as long as he promised to spit it into a cup and not on the floor.

Roger caught my eye, winked, and slipped out of the room. It was time for the big surprise.

A few minutes later, we all heard a soft winnie through the open window. Gus' face went slack with shock and recognition. Then, as Roger, leading Lightning, came around the corner of the building, Gus struggled to sit up. Tears streamed down his cheeks. Two of the nurses hurried to help him.

Roger led Lightning right up to the window, which we opened as far as we could. For a full fifteen minutes, Gus rubbed the horse's muzzle and whispered to him in a language only the two of them could understand.

At last the strain became too much for him. His hand fell slack at his side and his eyes started to roll back. The nurses helped him lie down while I closed the window and Roger led Lightning away.

Before I left Gus in the care of his family, I went to the head of the bed and put my hand on his shoulder. "Good birthday?" I asked.

He couldn't manage any speech, but he gave me his special, brown-toothed smile.

"All right," I said, leaning down to kiss his cheek, "I'll see you next week, then. Be good."

I never saw Gus again.

He slipped away just before midnight while Roger held his hand and the rest of the children crowded around the bed. The nurse who attended Gus's death told me that he had died with a smile on his face.

A few months later, Roger called to tell me that Lightning had passed away from old age. "I've never believed much in life after death," he said, "but I'm going to pretend that Dad and Lightning are together again. Does that sound dumb?"

"No," I said softly. "Not dumb at all."

I can't speak for what happens after the heart stops beating, but I do know that when Gus died, he was a happy man. He had his chewing tobacco, his family, and his beloved gelding. He would never have presumed to ask for anything more.

Afterword

A few months ago, a nurse and I went to the home of a potential patient and his family to provide information on hospice. "No one is signing anything today," the patient said sharply. "I don't want to be sold anything. I just have some questions."

The patient was angry and afraid. He had just turned fifty years old, and he simply couldn't bear to believe that not even one of his doctors could hold out hope for a new treatment for his cancer. "I'm not ready to stop fighting yet," he said. His wife and adult son sat on the couch and wept silently.

The patient, Justin, had a beautiful little brown and white terrier, Screwball, who sat by his chair and listened to the whole conversation with an almost human-like concern.

The nurse and I took turns stroking the terrier's fur and scratching his ears as we explained why the different treatments Justin wanted would likely hasten his death more than simply allowing nature to take its course.

When we had answered all of Justin's questions, he sat with his elbows resting on his knees and his head slumped between his shoulders. "I guess that's it, then," he said, more to himself than to anyone else in the room.

After a few more minutes, he straightened up with the raw courage of a man about to face torture and put a hand on the terrier's head. "Let's do it," he said. "Let's get that paperwork signed so I can start this thing."

"Justin, are you sure?" I asked. "We'd love to take care of you, but you said you didn't want to sign anything today. It's fine if you need more time to think…"

"No, I have all the information I need," he said. "It's silly to have you come out two days in a row because I'm an indecisive old fool. Let's get started now."

"As long as you're sure…"

"Young lady, you're the only sales person I've ever met who tried to talk herself *out* of a sale."

"But I'm not a sales person," I said, swiftly sorting out the few pages that required Justin's signature. "I'm a social worker."

"That explains it, then," he said with a good-natured laugh. He hastily looked the papers over and scrawled his name. The nurse whisked him off to the bedroom to do a physical assessment, and I went over to the couch to ask Justin's wife and son if they had any questions.

His wife, Shirley, smiled at me. "You do know why he decided to sign those papers today?" she said.

I shook my head. "He seemed pretty set against it when we arrived."

"It's because you and the nurse were nice to the dog. Anybody who is big hearted enough to realize that our dog might be upset and go out of your way to comfort it…that's who we want to provide Justin's care."

"As far as I'm concerned," I said, "Screwball is part of the family, too."

Justin remains on our hospice service. His cancer, although it will ultimately cause his death, is slow growing, and he is still able to do many of the things he enjoys, like taking Screwball for short walks or loading up the family in his car for a drive in the country.

Sometimes, he questions the wisdom of being on hospice, and holds out hope that a treatment for his disease must exist somewhere. He and I have sifted through newspaper articles, notices of clinical trials, and even a couple of obviously quack-cure solicitations. So far, nothing has shown promise.

Each time our efforts come up empty, Justin scratches Screwball under the chin and says, "Well, old boy, we did our best, didn't we?"

And the terrier, as if knowing exactly what is expected of him, puts his paws on Justin's knees and stares kindly and deeply into his master's eyes until the worry and sadness begin to dissipate like snow clouds giving way to warm sunlight.